THE
HUSBAND AND WIFE
BOOK

"Then you will call upon Me and go and pray to Me,
and I will listen to you. And you will seek Me and find Me,
when you search for Me with all your heart ..."
Jeremiah 29: 12-13

By Robin Williams

To order additional copies of this book,
email Robin Williams at robin@thehusbandandwifeclass.com.

This book is dedicated to

Ray

the best friend I have ever had,
a gift from God
my husband for life,
the one I love growing old with!

And

Mark,

our son,
A gift from God
whom we love beyond measure!

To God be the glory
for HIS TRUTH!

May we never stop walking in His Word!

THE HUSBAND AND WIFE BOOK
Reviews & Recommendations

The personal and intimate transparency of this book connects with the reader and reassures us that what we experience in our personal lives is normal and we are not alone. The strong and underlying communicated message is that there is a worldly way, and a godly way. You as the reader are confronted to make a choice, because you can't have it both ways. I read my Bible on a consistent basis, however this study has enlightened my wisdom and knowledge on how to have a godly marriage. I highly recommend this book.

Chip, Virginia

Thanks again for providing this class right when we needed it most. Once again, God's timing is ALWAYS best!

Phil and Suzanne, Virginia

I fully endorse and recommend this class for any new couple considering marriage, those who are newly married, and those that have been married for years. This class brings certain truths of God into perspective and re-enforces God's purpose for marriage and the roles that each partner plays in the marriage. God's role, husband's role, and wife's role – all together they are a team and as God's word says in Ecc. 4:12 "... a cord of three strands is not easily broken." So if your marriage is not what you thought it should be or is not what God thinks it should be, this class is for you and your spouse. It is never too late. Take it and I assure you that your marriage will be better for it. God bless.

Charlie and Joyce, Virginia

I recommend this class to everyone because I know it works. To the One who created marriage and wrote the Bible, it is the only way to a successful marriage. You must first want it and surrender to His Way to have it. A true miracle. This class can get you there.

M. Dodd, Virginia

When I read a book and it makes me laugh, cry, and get mad, I know I am in the middle of something good. There were things I learned I didn't like but needed to hear. It was indeed an answer to prayers. Truth that is transparent and God inspired. Down-to-earth examples with vulnerability that helps you relate and move forward. So thankful for this nugget!

Angie, Virginia

I like this book! It is Biblical and on-point as it goes straight to the need of people. I feel a lot of what is on the market today is centered on "fixing issues" rather than focusing on the relationship with God. This study keeps people God focused.

Pastor K. Gowin, Kentucky

TABLE OF CONTENTS

FOREWORD

The book you are holding in your hand is a true story. I know because I have lived it. If you will do the work, it will not only change your marriage, it will make it better than you could ever imagine.

Robin and I have been married for 35 years. I have watched her sit at the feet of God every morning. It does not matter what is going on in our lives. In good times and bad, on speaking terms or not (especially in the beginning), at home or on vacation, weekdays or weekends, money in the bank or no money in the bank - it doesn't matter. She sits at His feet every morning. That has not only affected her life, it has eternally influenced my life, our marriage, and our home in a huge way. Our son grew up seeing his mother read her bible everyday. That had an eternal effect on his life.

This book is the result of years of Robin seeking God's truths about marriage and relationships. The most important relationship, as you will soon see, is a personal one with Christ. This book focuses on getting that relationship right. Once that happens, He teaches how to get the marriage right.

The things you will learn and apply will make your home a place you enjoy, your family the most important people in your life, and your marriage better than ever. As we have taught this class over the last 20 years, we have found that our marriage is no different than most marriages. Please take it seriously.

Thank you, Robin, for leading me and Mark to Christ. Thank you for sharing the wisdom God has imparted to you as you have devoted your life to HIM. Being in love with you is a blessing and great way to live my life.

Ray

WEEK
One

Introduction

W elcome to the Husband and Wife Class. We are Ray and Robin Williams. As of this writing, we are approaching 35 years of marriage. That is quite an accomplishment considering we did not think we were going to make it past year two! What you are about to experience is the process that saved our marriage. Early on I had this terrible feeling we had made a huge mistake. I found out a lot of people feel that way. The good news is the marriage doesn't have to end. The sad news is, all too often marriages do end.

The material you are about to study over the next 12-weeks, covers about 18 years of a journey God took us on. Two years into our marriage I started asking God to do something to fix us. I wanted to find a book I could read that would make it all better. I went to the Christian bookstores and picked up every book I could find on being a wife. They all said the same thing. The husband was the head of the wife and the wife was supposed to be submissive. I stopped reading those books. I had not grown enough in my Christian walk to even want to hear that non sense, much less try to believe it. I had no intentions of living that out, and knew my life would never look like that. Tired of searching, I desperately called out to God one morning in my quiet time. I pleaded with HIM to write the book I was so desperately looking for, using me and my experiences. He did! You are holding that book in your hands!

Since we are Christians, this study is strictly based on Christian principles. All research comes from the Bible. All scripture is taken from the New King James version except where otherwise noted. There are a few definitions taken from Webster's New World Dictionary. We invite anyone to read and do this study. You do not have to be a Christian to read it, but it will help to be a Christian if you are going to do the study. We believe you have to be a Christian with the Holy Spirit of God residing in your heart if you want to live it. God is the only one who can transform us into the people He created us to be. Everything we do is supposed to bring honor and glory to God. HE ordained marriage. We do not automatically know how to have Christian marriages or how to honor God and each other in our relationship. We have to learn that. That is what this study teaches.

When you get it right at home, you do not have to pretend you are something you are not, outside of the home. While this material started out being for wives only, God has continued to lead Ray and I to share this with husbands and wives. We believe healthy marriages yield healthy families, homes, churches, and communities. A Godly marriage is a venue of hope. Our hope is Christ. He is always the answer and HIS way is the only way. Our starting place is with God, inside our own individual hearts, inside our own home. We pray for your heart and your home. We are still on our journey and we still face challenges. I still pull this study out even when we are not teaching a class or mentoring a couple because I have to be reminded over and over what scripture tells us about a marriage and a home that honors God. Then I have to decide to live it out by hiding His Word in my heart so I will not sin against HIM. We pray this study will do as much for you and your family as it has for us and ours. May God bless you on your journey.

WEEK
Two

Am I the only one who feels like this?

People say the first year of marriage is the toughest. It is during the first year of living together that you get to find out all kinds of "hidden" things about each other. That is when she learns her husband might not look (or smell) as good after a night of sleep as he did when he used to pick her up for a date. That is when he learns the same about her. It is during this time we get introduced to each other's habits. It is possible that one or two of those habits border on being repulsive. You might not have even known "it" existed prior to getting married. Now you wonder how you could have missed it. It is also possible that what you used to find irresistible and think was so funny and cute is now the very thing you can't stand! For example, maybe your spouse is a talker. That might have been the characteristic you liked the most in the beginning. Now, you wish he/she would just be quiet!

She had no idea he would be the type to leave his dirty clothes on the floor. He had no idea she wouldn't enjoy doing the laundry, cleaning the house, and waiting on him. She certainly didn't know he made so much noise when he ate cereal because she doesn't remember him ever eating cereal when they dated. Neither of you could foresee the financial challenges. She thought he was still going to pay for everything and her money was still going to be her money. She liked going out to eat and had no idea he was going to look for a home cooked meal every night. And how about all the work and responsibility that falls on one or both of you around the house? You work all day, come home, and now have a second thankless job. It is not uncommon for most of the household responsibilities to migrate towards one person. This can cause resentment because whichever one of "you" it is, starts thinking all your spouse has to do is go to work and come home, while you do everything else.

Maybe you have been married 10 years or more and while the aforementioned challenges have already been worked through, you find other things that are driving you apart. Maybe you no longer share the same interests. Maybe he's a hunter and you are a hunting widow. Maybe she's a shopper and you're working two jobs just to feed her habits. Maybe you both spend too much time with friends and not enough time at home. Maybe deceitful patterns have seeped into the relationship and perhaps there are trust or distrust issues you find yourselves having to deal with.

Maybe there are in-law challenges, and/or too much extended family involvement. Maybe you are just so disappointed with the way things have turned out that you've given up on the relationship. When that happens you usually give up on even thinking about trying to please each other.

Are you the only one who feels like you do? No! It is amazing how much we really are alike. It is our human nature. We all tend to fall in love with whatever or whomever we perceive is meeting our need or needs. When you met your prospective spouse, chances are you were either living with your parents and your mother was still meeting most of your practical needs, i.e. cleaning the house, doing the laundry, cooking the meals, etc. Perhaps you were living on your own and had only yourself to worry about. If the laundry got done, great, if not, there was always something else to wear – or you could go buy to wear! There was no one to answer to. When you started dating, it is a good chance the only thing you were concerned about was "having fun!"

It could be the only needs you were aware of were the emotional needs. You were probably much more interested in someone to spend time with, laugh with, go to the movies, dance, talk, share a moonlit evening, romantic dinner, hold you, understand you, listen to you, think you were perfect, etc., etc. While your parents may have been the ones to meet your physical and practical needs prior to moving out, your mate was the special person who met those emotional needs before you were married. With time, things change. All of the sudden you feel like your house has become like the one you left when you lived with your parents. Now that you are doing the cooking, the cleaning, paying the bills, taking care of the children, and all of the things that come with making a living and running a home, you find yourself daydreaming about someone to "share" time with. You long for someone to laugh with, go to the movies with, dance with, talk with, share a moonlit evening, have a romantic dinner, understand you, tell you how wonderful you are, how special you are, hold you, kiss you, listen to you, and think you are perfect. Unfortunately, now, that person just might not be your spouse!

If any of this sounds the least bit familiar, please know you are not alone. I know from personal experience that you can not only feel this way, you start feeling guilty about feeling this way. You try to suppress the feelings. You try to masquerade the feelings. You have a war going on inside yourself and you can't put your finger on the problem. You've been able to pin the problem down to him or her in general and everything he or she does in specific! We know how you feel. We have been there and can still go back there if we are not careful. Here is the scenario. You are both unhappy, maybe even miserable and the children are lost in all of it. Perhaps one or both of you wants out of the marriage, and the children just want mom and dad to like each other. If you are at that point or are on that path, I have great news for you. You are going to get out. In one of three ways, you are going to get out. A life change is just a decision away. You will make one of the following choices:

- You will either divorce ... or

- Decide to stay together and live a life of miserable existence, you with your life, your spouse with theirs and neither the two shall pass ... or

- You will decide to turn your marriage over to God and allow HIM to build a new marriage.

That's it! Those are the only choices.

In America, depending on which statistical data you read (and there is no shortage of data in cyber land), between 40% and 60% of new marriages will eventually end in divorce. There is also data that says the Christian divorce rate is not much better. We will talk more about that as we get further into this study. Whether it is 40% or 60% the fact is there are many divorces. Perhaps an even more sobering thought is people bypassing marriage altogether. It is culturally acceptable these days to live together, and proliferate outside of marriage. If you do decide to get married, the point is around half of those that marry will divorce. It is a good chance you may have already divorced and are in a second or third marriage. If that is your situation, depending on how long you've been in this marriage, it is possible that you are experiencing some familiar challenges. Did you just marry the wrong person? What exactly does that mean? Who is the right person? The truth is none of us really know the person we marry. We might think we know them, but it is probably more accurate to say we marry the person we have created them in our minds to be. It is likely we have imagined them to be someone or something they are not, and perhaps never could be. As the masks come off (and they will) we become pretty disappointed in each other. It is possible we find ourselves wondering if we really love each other anymore. That is when we start thinking about divorce. After all, don't we deserve to be happy?

I like this one, "I love him/her but am not in love any longer. So the entitlement attitude sets in. "I deserve to be happy!" "There must be somebody out there that I can love and be loved back!" We divorce. We drag the children through goodness only knows what. We finally meet that perfect person (their ex didn't understand them either!), and for some reason we think their story is so sad - yet it is the same story your ex is out there telling somebody about you! Now you marry the "right" person. The children get to live with somebody else's mother/father. Your "ex" is living with somebody else's children. What is that doing to the children? What kind of society is that creating? Two to five years into this marriage, there might be another child or two, and all of the sudden, you are questioning if you married the right person, AGAIN!

If I suggested that all relationships are basically the same, would you hear me out? I have no scientific research that backs that up, but I have countless testimonies that validate that statement. Did I just happen upon people with the same story? Is my experience some sort of coincidence? No. People are people and they are pretty predictable. Before I go any further, let me make a disclaimer. I am not talking about an abusive marriage. Nor am I talking about a marriage that is constantly dealing with infidelity. Both of those situations need counseling I am not qualified to give. If that describes your marriage, you are welcome to do this study and could possibly find it helpful, but I would suggest you seek professional help. If your situation involves abusive and/or life threatening acts, I would encourage you to seek safety for you and your children first, then professional help. This study will focus on what I like to call an "irritable" marriage.

What is an irritable marriage? It is the one that I have already described. It is the marriage that has lost its "shine" – no more excitement. It's the one that finds you and your spouse with less and less in common. It's the one that leaves you rolling your eyes because your spouse has told that same sorry story again and again. It's the one that has left you disappointed it hasn't turned out the way you thought it should have. It might even be the one you have decided to end. If you have been able to relate to anything I've said so far, can I dare suggest an irritable marriage is exactly like your marriage? That surely described my marriage.

If your decision is to divorce, please make sure you are not doing that because "there has to be someone out there that can make you happy!" That thought process is the main ingredient for another irritable marriage. It is not someone else's responsibility to make you happy. And how terrible would it be to divorce, remarry, and find out 3 years into the new marriage that your previous marriage wasn't so bad after all? I am not making light of that. The truth is, someone could be reading this right now thinking that very thought. My heart goes out to you because you just didn't know the truth. That is what we are going to learn in this study, THE TRUTH! While your heart might be breaking right now, just see this through, and hopefully you will never find yourself in the same situation again. One truth is, there may be someone you could fall in love (or lust) with but that doesn't make him or her the right person. The responsibility for two people who are mature enough to fall in love and get married is to make the marriage right, not the person.

Let's talk about the second decision. You decide to stay together, maybe for the sake of the children. Maybe for no other reason than you just can't afford to leave. Whatever the reason, your decision is to stay in the marriage, but not necessarily work at making it work. Friend, that is a miserable existence. If you have been living with that decision for any length of time, you know exactly what I mean. Just in case you are not sure if that is what you've decided, let me give you some examples of that type of marriage. My guess is your age is somewhere between 20 and 60 something. If you are in your 60's, it's been my observation (I will know if I am right or not as soon as I get there – which isn't too terribly far from now!), that your marriage is probably similar to the friends you are closest to. You might not have declared out loud that "you were not going to work on your marriage and that you were deciding to live miserable inside of it" but your actions have spoken it for you. You laugh and joke with your friends about husband and wife things, namely negative things. It's a good chance you live very separate lives, with separate friends, separate likes, etc. etc. Beyond the children and grandchildren you never developed a life together. An attempt to do anything different at this point is not even thought of anymore. Now, the other end of the spectrum, you're in your 20's. Depending on how long you have been married, you might be having thoughts like "is this what life is supposed to be like?" You might have a child or two. It is quite possible you are entering a time of uncertainty about what you have gotten yourself into, but it's not likely you are resolved to living like this the rest of your life. Today's culture teaches "you deserve to be happy" and your whole life is ahead of you. You might be thinking your spouse will surely change soon, or you might be looking elsewhere for someone else to fit the bill. It is just too soon to know what your decision will be. The ones who are keenly aware of a decision to be made are in their 30's, 40's and 50's.

Here is the scenario. You both went to school, high school, and/or college. You graduated, dated, married, had a family, bought the new cars and the house, have your jobs or careers, and are either just beginning to settle into a lifestyle (30+), or you have been established in that lifestyle for some time (40's – 50's). With the spouse, the house, the cars, the jobs, the children, you have attained all the things you never dreamt past. Now what? I do not know what all little boys spend their growing up days dreaming of. Having a son, I sure remember his interest in playing army, being a detective, a policeman, a fireman, playing baseball, soccer, and golf, any of those things could have been pursuable dreams. I do know that the girlfriends I grew up with spent our days dreaming of getting married, having a family, and playing house. I am not sure how much thought is given to life beyond those things. After all, what does a child, a teen, or a young adult know about life beyond those things? Succeeding in an education, job, career, business, getting married, car purchase, house purchase, and having children are incredible accomplishments in and of themselves. How were we supposed to know there might come a day when those things weren't going to be "enough?" Once the thrill of all of "that" wears off, (and it does), and once the disappointment of not "becoming something you thought you would" is reality, what then? Life certainly doesn't teach us how to be prepared for such disappointment does it? Often we think another job, child, pet, house, car, boat, or new spouse is going to fill that ache in our heart and make like worth living again!

Is any of this resonating? No? How about this? You get up Monday thru Friday and go your separate ways. You have each learned where the other draws the line, and you have settled into a lifestyle that is not necessarily unbearable, but neither is it a growing, thriving, thrilling, fulfilling marital relationship. You have moments of "togetherness" but for the most part he has his life and you have yours. The children may or may not be the focus of both of your lives and they may or may not bring you together. You both might be very involved in church activities. They might not necessarily be activities that bring you together. (Just an aside, I remember when I had my melt down – age 37 more about that later – my husband and I were very involved in church activities, but not together! BEWARE!) As God took me through a purging process, He made me keenly aware of how families can be pulled apart even at church if priorities are out of whack! That's not necessarily the fault of the church, in fact to the contrary. It is the responsibility of the husband and wife to "tend to the marriage" as it is spelled out by God, and it helps when the church is on board with that!

It is a natural process to grow apart. That takes little to no effort. It takes effort to grow together in a loving relationship! I have often said I fell in love with Ray because of the things he did and because of the way he made me feel, and I fell out of love with him because of the things he did and the way he made me feel! Can anybody relate to that statement? It is not surprising or uncommon with time for resentment to build, good feelings to turn bad, like turns to dislike, love is seemingly lost, irresistible is replaced with irritation. We resolve in our hearts that it is easier to live with the enemy we know rather than travel into something new. That is a miserable existence, but in an odd sort of way it offers some security. At least we know "what to" or "what not to" expect. After all, mom and dad are living under the same roof and the whole family has grown accustomed to the lifestyle. All outside appearances give the impression all is well. There might be times when you think you are going to go crazy because your spouse does that one thing AGAIN that you just can't get over and you feel so ill towards them you can't ever imagine feeling good about them or the relationship ever again. Perhaps trust has become truce and where there once were "hearts of fire" there now needs to be a "cease fire." There is a fine line between love and hate and you straddle that line every couple of months.

Need more? How about this? There is not much conversation beyond what you absolutely have to discuss. You learn to live without having to discuss much. In fact, often, your spouse is the last to know something he/she should have been the first to know, and you play it off, when busted, by saying "I thought I told you?" You know you didn't tell them because that would have meant you would have had to carry on a conversation! You might even go to church on Sundays and Wednesdays and put on that happy couple face. All the while you are dying inside. I could go on and on with many more examples, but those of you who have made the decision to live in a miserable existence have read enough now to know if you are there or not. You don't know what to do or how to change it. Some days you want to get out of it, even if it's a mental divorce, and other days you are not so sure. Friend, if you are like us, and I am sure one or two of you are, you find yourself wondering "how in this world could two people who loved each other so much find themselves in such a mess?" We have learned the answer to that question through the years (with intentional search I might add!), and before you get to the end of this study, you will too. It has been my personal observation that a LARGE percentage of the married couples (who do not divorce) live in this category. Only a precious few ever make the third or last (best and toughest!) choice.

What does giving up the fight and turning the marriage over to God mean? First I need to make another disclaimer. The study you are about to undertake is based on the Christian Faith. I do not know what other faiths believe or teach about the marital relationship. I am a Christian and everything you read about marriage according to this study will be based on the Christian faith. The Christian faith teaches that God ordained marriage between one man and one woman. (Genesis 2:21-25). They were intended to be naked and not ashamed. In a spiritual sense, that says to me "they should be able to know all there is to know about each other, bearing it all before one another, and not be ashamed." Sadly, we become ashamed because we no longer strive to become one flesh, and we turn away from God and each other. We start missing out on the blessings of God at that point and we block those blessings from flowing to future generations. Ray and I did not start out with that belief. It has been a process that has brought us to that belief. We will take you on that journey if you care to go.

Two years into our marriage, I wanted out! In just two short years we had destroyed something that neither of us would have believed possible. Our love for each other was so strong (so we thought) that nothing could ever tear us apart. I never dreamed we would tear each other apart. We didn't mean to do that. It was a natural progression that took place in a short amount of time. We had discussed the "divorce" option a couple of times and had not completely ruled it out. There was one thing that kept nagging at me. I knew God hated divorce. I just didn't know why. I also knew we were miserable. Surely God would prefer an amicable divorce over a miserable marriage wouldn't HE? Especially if children were involved, which they weren't at that point, but if they were, wouldn't it be better for them if mom and dad were apart and friends, rather than together and fighting? That's what the world will tell you. That's even what Christians who have never studied biblical marriage will tell you. That's what people who make up God to be what "makes sense" will tell you, and that's what people who believe the only thing that's important about marriage is that you "are happy" will tell you. Friend, be careful who you seek counsel from!

There was really only one reason we did not divorce. GOD. We were both Christians when we got married. We took our vows "until death do we part" very seriously. As tempting as it was to call it quits, I could not break that vow. We decided to counsel with our pastor. He told us that before he would agree to counsel us, we had to agree to get the "divorce" word out of our vocabulary. We had to burn the bridge to the divorce option, as it could not be an option. Beyond that, I really cannot remember what else he told us or how short lived our sessions were. We opted to view divorce as "not an option." I am glad we did. Not because that made everything ok and we lived happily ever after. Rather, because it forced us to seek other means of resolve.

It is better for you that our lives didn't improve just because we made the decision not to divorce. If just making that decision would have taken care of all our problems, this wouldn't be much of a study and you might not have the same experience. We continued down our miserable existence path. Our pastor offered a marriage class and we took it. It was based on the book by Gary Smalley "Love is a decision" and I hated it! As much as I might agree with the author now that love is a decision, I wanted no parts of it then. You see, I was in so much pain. I was so angry and full of resentment that my life was not what I thought it should be or would be, and in my mind, it was all my husband's fault. The only thing I was picking up from the "Love is a decision" book was how we were supposed to honor each other. Honor each other? I wasn't even sure we liked each other! It was way too much for me to digest.

I did my own search. I visited the Christian bookstores. Every husband/wife book I read seemed to suggest I needed to pay attention to what "he" needed. I couldn't for the life of me find one that brought me comfort (mainly because I had no idea what a biblical marriage was all about, and primarily because I was starting with "me" when I should have been starting with God – but we will have that discussion soon enough!). I was looking for the book that was going to get me to the starting line. The starting line for me was where I could at least feel like I wanted to make it work. I had to get rid of the resentment. I could not stomach the books that were telling me I needed to be a submissive wife. I didn't want to be a wife at all. Finally in total desperation I cried out to God. I pleaded with Him to write that book I was so desperately looking for through me, using me and my experiences. He did. You are holding that book in your hands right now. I wish I could tell you I had you in mind as I wrote this. I didn't. I had me in mind. But more importantly, I believe God had you in mind and that's why this is in print.

God has been faithful to answer every question I have ever taken to Him about marriage. I said in the beginning that this is a journey. It does not happen overnight. I fully surrendered my marriage to God. I asked Him to please take the marriage that we had made such a mess of and turn it into what He intended it to be. I confessed that we had totally destroyed the marriage and each other in the process. I sensed God's grace. I sensed His forgiveness, and I sensed a burden lifted. The marriage wasn't repaired, it was replaced. Since that time, it has been, and continues to be, built according to God's plan for marriage.

We still have our challenges, but we have learned how to handle them differently. God has shown us how to build our marriage on truth - His Truth! Our lives are totally different today than they were years ago when we were entertaining the choice of divorce. We moved beyond that choice, lived briefly in the decision to live miserably together the rest of our lives, and finally decided to turn our marriage over to God. When I asked God to turn our marriage into what He would have it become, to be honest, Ray didn't know what I was doing because we didn't talk very much in those days. He knows now of course and we are still on the journey we are inviting you to start.

Will your spouse change? I cannot guarantee that he/she will. I can guarantee you will change, if you purpose in your heart to allow God to change you. Will that mean you will always and forever be happy with your spouse? No. It means, you will learn how to live a fulfilling life inside your marriage, if done according to God's way, which is found in His Word. God is much more interested in our holiness and obedience than He is about our earthly and worldly happiness. The world we live in, which we will talk more about later, cons us into believing that being happy is all that we need to be concerned with. Marriage is so much more than that. God has a purpose for marriage. We will discover that purpose in a few weeks. That purpose extends way beyond the two people in the marriage. The way we handle our marriages affects generations. As

Christians, we are responsible to those that went before us, our peers, and those that come after us. When we live according to God's commands, we are promised God's blessings, not just for you but for your family as well. How can I guarantee that? God blesses obedience.

I want to encourage you to make the third choice. Please don't divorce. Please don't live miserably for the rest of your life. Please make the only decision that will bring you victory. Give your marriage to God and let Him do with it what He will. I have never regretted making that decision. Does your husband / wife have to make the same decision? As already mentioned, I didn't tell Ray about the decision I made. I just started seeking God quietly. God has shown me incredible things about marriage. My focus has been on my role as a Christian woman and wife. In the process, I have been shown a great deal about the role of the Christian husband. Through the years we have started making progress as we have accepted the roles and the characteristics bit by bit, as God has impressed them upon our hearts. It takes study, commitment, desire, and patience. Yes there are times when you feel like you have taken two steps forward and three steps backwards. But the important part is you've made the decision to be different. You have made the decision to move forward. You have made a decision that honors God. God will bless you and your family.

In this book you will find each week has a five day format with study activities to start you on your journey. For the next five days, you will be able to examine your life and determine right where you are. Please allow this time to be yours. This is for you. It is not for your spouse or your children, although they will benefit beyond anything you can imagine if you will see this through to completion. This study is about getting your heart healed and healthy, then your home will be changed.

You are not the only one who feels like you do. This week you will take time to understand exactly how you feel; take a look at who you are talking to about how you feel; get a glimpse of your speech patterns and how they might be doing untold damage; take a look at the advice you have been given and who is giving it to you; and lastly, take a look at just how much God cares about all of this. The amount of time and sincerity you spend with this will determine your individual outcome and success. My prayer is that you will open your heart and soul to God for total renewal and restoration. You might want to get a spiral notebook to aid you on this journey. Enjoy!

Day One – How do you feel?

1) In the introduction to this week's lesson, we looked at three paths a marriage can take. Are you on one of those paths? Explain your answer.

2) Describe your marriage as it is right now.

3) Describe your idea of the ideal marriage.

4) What do you do to contribute to the "health" of your marriage?

5) What does your spouse do to contribute to the "health" of your marriage?

6) Do you love your spouse? Explain your answer.

7) How should a husband and wife love each other?

Spend the remainder of your time in this study today, writing a private letter to God in your journal telling Him exactly how you feel about yourself, your spouse, your children (if applicable), and your life. If you are ready, ask Him to take your marriage and turn it into what He would have it become. If you are not ready to make that request, just spend time in prayer asking God to show you any areas of your heart that He would like to talk to you about.

Day Two - Who do you talk to?

Yesterday you hopefully spent time writing about how you feel. Today, we want to focus on who you talk to about how you feel. It is very dangerous to give sensitive information to someone who is not going to treat the information in a responsible way. What do I mean by responsible? If you are talking with anyone about your "problems" and they are not directing you to God's Word for resolve and restoration, (in other words, they are not giving Godly counsel), you need to stop talking to them about your marital problems. It doesn't mean you cannot maintain your friendship with them, (unless of course it is an inappropriate relationship with a member of the opposite sex - that is taboo and we will talk more about that later in the study). It means your marital problems probably shouldn't be discussed with them. Why? It is a good chance they are agreeing with you, which probably makes for a negative conversation. Consequently that is making matters worse! Let me give you an example.

You call your friend on the phone and start the conversation by saying "you will not believe what my husband / wife did last night!" Then you go on talking negatively about something your spouse has done. All the while your friend is offering advice about what they would say or do if their spouse ever did that. By the time you hang up, your spouse is not only a jerk for what he/she did last night, you have probably dug deep into the garbage bag and pulled out six or seven things he/she has done over the last couple of years. Now the situation is ten times worse than it was when you started the conversation. It is a good chance your friend has compared some of the "dumb" things his/ her spouse has done too and you both hang up really angry with your spouses. Negativity breeds negativity. That type of conversation will do more harm than you can imagine. That type of counsel is ungodly. If you want to start seeing a positive change in your marriage, you need to pay close attention to who you are talking to and what you are saying.

1) Who do you talk to about your husband / wife / marriage?

2) Who talks to you about their spouse / marriage?

3) How do you feel after you talk to someone about your spouse? Explain your answer.

4) Read Psalm 1:1-6.

   a) What does it say about the person who walks "not" in the counsel of the ungodly? (vs. 1)

   b) Who should we "not" walk in the same path with? (vs. 1)
      Or sit in the same seat with? (vs. 1).

   c) Where should our delight be? (vs2)

   d) What should we be meditating in day and night? (vs.2)

e) What will happen to the person who delights in the law of the Lord and meditates in His law day and night? (vs. 3)

f) What happens to the ungodly? (vs. 4-6)

5) Perhaps you have never given any thought to who you choose to talk with about your spouse. Changing what you share and who you share things with could very well improve your marital relationship immediately. For one week, why don't you purpose in your heart to not talk to anyone negatively about your spouse. Does that mean he/she won't do anything that you wouldn't love to tell somebody about? No. It just means you are resolving to take a more responsible approach to the private things you will share. It also means you will eliminate any opportunity for Satan to get a hold of the conversation and make it worse. Make a promise to yourself that you will not speak negatively about your spouse or marriage to anyone for the rest of this week. Write your promise.

6) Come back to this page at the end of this week and record any improvements you may have noticed as a direct result of sticking to that promise.

Let me encourage you to stop talking negatively to anyone about your spouse and your marriage. Let me encourage you to be blessed because you only walk in the counsel of the Godly. Let me encourage you to be "like a tree planted by the rivers of water that brings forth its fruit in its season, whose leaf will not wither, and in whatever you do you will prosper."

Pray about who you should seek counsel from regarding your spouse and/or marital issues. We all need a mentor or someone we can trust to give us responsible Godly counsel. If you are involved in a church family, pray and ask God to lead you to a mentor relationship with an older person. There is nothing more renewing than being able to spend time talking to a believer who loves the Lord and who's life bears good fruit. They will always lead you to God's Word for guidance and encouragement. I have found that if I am talking with someone who I know loves our Lord and HIS Word, I am much more gracious in my speech. My words are much kinder and more carefully chosen. End this session by praying about a mentor and writing in your journal about how you think seeking Godly counsel could benefit you in your marriage.

Day Three – What is your manner of speech?

Yesterday we talked about who you talk to. Today we are going to talk about what you say, or, your manner of speech. What we say and how we say it can either build up an individual or it can tear them down. Our speech is usually a manifestation of our thoughts. In most cases, we say exactly what we think. There are cases where we speak without thinking and there are times when we wish we would not have said something we did. But, for the most part, we know exactly what we are saying as we "speak our minds" so the saying goes. All too often, our speech is not edifying. Women love to talk. It is our nature. Most men do not talk a lot. It is their nature. Have you ever thought about how much men and women tear each other down over things that each of them are naturally? We take each other's God given gifts and use them against the other one. Let me explain.

It is not uncommon to hear women complaining about how a man can only do one thing at a time. Men are naturally one tasked oriented. Because of that characteristic they are not easily side tracked. The down side to that, from a woman's point of view, is they might get little accomplished. In my house, we call it being "locked in" on something. My husband and my son both demonstrate that trait. I, on the other hand, can be talking on the phone, folding clothes, stop and feed the dog, start another load of clothes, empty the trash and go look up a Bible verse for the friend I am talking to on the phone, all without batting an eyelid! You can too. Women are naturally multi-tasked. The down side to that is we are often sidetracked and can seemingly work all day and get little accomplished. Often, we do not see those traits as strengths. Instead we take those differences and abuse each other.

Put a frustrated married woman on the phone with a frustrated married girlfriend that will listen, and before you know it both of their spouses are the scum of the earth! That manner of speech is degrading. You might argue that while it may be degrading, isn't it true? It might be true, but do we have to be so brutal in our speech? Would our manner of speech be the same if Jesus were there listening to us? God engineered us all. Satan would have us tear each other down because of a strength God intended to be a blessing. Men do the same thing to women. Because women can do multiple things at one time, we tend to think men should be able to do that too. Sometimes, (probably most of the time), the orders we tend to "bark" at our husbands are viewed by them as "nagging" instead of cries for help. Consequently, women think men can't do anything and men think women nag. We live defeated lives.

The Bible speaks a lot about manner of speech. If we are using our tongues to tear one of God's creations down, it is evil. My husband is one of God's creations. I have no right to speak evil of him - to anyone! In fact, one of the characteristics of love, according to God, is it thinks no evil. Demonstrating love for my husband means I am not supposed to think evil towards him. We will talk more about that later in this study. We are called by God to a life of blessing. God wants to fellowship with us and He wants His love to shine through us. He wants to expand His Kingdom through us. Our lives should bring honor to God, especially in our marriages. One way to do that is to make sure our speech is not degrading.

1) Read 1st Peter 3: 8-12.

   We are instructed to treat one another in five ways. List them. (vs.8)

   a) _____

   b) _____

   c) _____

   d) _____

   e) _____

2) What are we told not to do? (vs. 9)

3) To the contrary of returning evil for evil and reviling for reviling, what are we supposed to do? And what were we called to? (vs. 9)

4) If you want to love life and see good days, what are you supposed to do? (vs.10,11)

5) The eyes of the Lord are on who? (vs.12)

6) Who does God hear? (vs. 12)

7) Who is the face of the Lord against? (vs.12)

Is speaking negative about your spouse an evil thing? God convicted me of speaking evil about my husband. I was spewing venom on one of God's created. I have kept a spiritual journal for years. There was a time in my life where every morning I started off by writing to God with complaints of Ray. What I didn't realize was God wasn't even listening to me according to 1st Peter 3:12. His eyes are on the righteous and His ears are open to their prayers. His face is against those who do evil. You say, oh come on Robin, do you really believe that? Yes I do. My husband was a Christian just like I was. What made me think God would hear me when all I was doing was complaining about one of His own? Look at the example of David and Saul. Why wouldn't David kill Saul when he had the chance? Because he couldn't touch one of God's anointed. David trusted God enough to know that God would deal with Saul. We have to trust God enough to know that if our spouse needs dealing with, God will do it. It wasn't my place (then or now!) to "deal" with my spouse. Revile means to use abusive language to or about someone. I was using abusive language to God about my husband. I don't think He was hearing me. I hope He wasn't!

The nature of my complaints against my husband were not necessarily things he was doing wrong. A lot of the complaints were simply things that irritated me. Throughout this study, we will learn how to determine what is an irritation versus a non-Christ like characteristic, and how to deal with each one appropriately. It is easy to label everything that irritates you as something that makes your spouse less-Christian than you, but that is a false image. We will learn more about false images over the next two weeks. When we take something that irritates us and try to turn it into something that we define as not being "of God" we run the risk of destroying our marriages, our children, our extended families, and each other. Dare I suggest that most of what you complain to your friends about are irritants? That is what I used to hear. I say used to because I will not listen to it any more. God has given me the strength through the years to be able to turn my face and ears against it. I will not participate in a conversation where the manner of speech is degrading and the subject matter is a person's faults. I will however, participate in a conversation where true resolve is being sought in God. There is quite a difference in the manner of speech being used, and the motive behind it. I learned a long time ago that I can't help a person whose motive is to belittle another person. I can, however, offer hope to a person who is seeking a resolve in marriage by seeking God.

For some reason, we think that being of one mind, having compassion for one another, loving as brothers, being tenderhearted, and being courteous, means acting that way towards everyone except our spouse! Peter had just finished specifically addressing husbands and wives when he gave those commands of conduct. Of course we are to treat our spouses that way. When I started practicing that, our marriage started changing. I believe most divorces would never take place if we simply changed the way we speak to each other. Something as simple as how we talk to one another could change the next generation for the good. Give some thought to the following questions as we finish this lesson.

8) On a scale from 1 to 10 (1 being the least degrading, 10 being the most), how would you rate the manner of speech you use towards your spouse when you are talking to a friend about something he/she does that irritates you? Explain your answer.

9) How would you describe your manner of speech towards your spouse while you are talking to him/her? Explain your answer.

10) For all of you brave hearts, ask your spouse to describe your manner of speech towards him/her. Record their answer.

11) For all of you **REALLY, REALLY** brave hearts, ask your spouse to tell you how it makes him/her feel when you discuss your marital situation (namely the negative things) with your friends. Record their answer.

You might not be ready to attempt those last two questions. It is okay if you are not. If you do ask your spouse to share his/her thoughts, be willing to just record the answers and not retaliate if they are not too positive. Ask God to prepare your heart for the answers and then just talk to God about them. Your spouse might see this as an opportunity to return some evil for evil, and if that is the case, ask God for a double dose of protection. It is very possible healing needs to take place in both of your hearts, so just listen and please do not let this add one more brick to the wall that now stands between you. Let it be a beginning of tearing the wall down.

Hopefully, you are beginning to realize the importance of your manner of speech. How we think and talk is very important to God. He is the one in whom we will find our strength and redemption. We might feel better for the moment if we unload our garbage on our friends who allow us to participate in that type of destructive talk, but we will never find strength or redemption in it. Nor will it be pleasing to God or helpful to our marriage.

12) Write out Psalm 19:14 and turn it into your prayer for the day.

Day Four – What type of advice have you been given?

It is not hard today to find advice on any subject! With the internet, you google it and you have all kinds of information instantly. The world is full of people giving advice! What type of advice have you been given? What type of advice do you seek and who do you seek it from?

Re-read Psalm 1. Refresh your memory by turning back to the things you wrote in Day Two about this passage of scripture. We are clearly to walk in the counsel of the Godly and delight in the law of the Lord, meditating in it day and night. In so doing, we will be like a tree planted (and rooted in sound instruction) by the rivers of water and will bring forth fruit in its season and everything we do will prosper!

1) Who do you get advice from on husband/wife/marriage issues?

2) Are those people, or is that person, rooted in the Word of God? Explain your answer.

3) Are those people, or is that person, married?   ____ yes   ____ no

   If no, have they ever been married?   ____ yes   ____ no

4) Has that person (or those people) ever been divorced?   ____ yes   ____ no

   If yes, how many times?   _____ times

5) How long have they been married or how long were they married?   _____

6) On what specific issues have you sought advice?

7) What type of advice have you been given?

8) Has the advice you have been given helped your marriage or hurt your marriage?
Explain your answer.

9) Would you say you have sought Godly counsel? ____ yes ____ no
Explain your answer.

10) Would you say the counsel you have received has been Godly? ____ yes ____ no
Explain your answer.

11) The world has advice for people who are unhappy in their marriage. Get divorced. Go find someone you can be happy with. Life is too short! Leave your spouse! You don't have to put up with that! That is not Godly counsel. Who we talk to, the way we talk to them, and the advice we take are all equally important. All three aspects, and how responsibly we handle them, will have a tremendous influence on our marriage.

Read and write Proverbs 14:1

The New King James version says: The wise woman builds her house, but the foolish pulls it down with her hands. Substitute the word "hands" with "mouth" and re-read the verse. Substitute the word "hands" with the words "negative thoughts" and re-read the verse. Substitute the word "hands" with the words "ungodly counsel" and re-read the verse.

... but the foolish pulls it down with their mouth

... but the foolish pulls it down with their negative thoughts

... but the foolish pulls it down with their ungodly counsel

Of course, a man can just as easily pull a family and household down with his hands, mouth, negative thoughts, and ungodly counsel. The "wise" build their homes. I know we all want to be counted as wise!

12) Read and write Proverbs 15:28

Please only seek counsel from someone whose life testifies to a solid relationship with God. A person who studies the Word of God is going to point you to the Word of God.

Day Five – Does God care about this?

There is nothing, in my opinion, more powerful and encouraging than a testimony given by someone about what God has done and is continuing to do in and through a person's life. We are all the same. We were all created in God's image (Genesis 1:27). It is sin that separates us from God. When we are walking in reconciled fellowship with Him, through the redemptive blood of our Lord and Savior Jesus Christ, we are fulfilled and whole. There is no joy like that of the one who is rightly related to God. It shows in all they do. But how about the days, hours, or moments we are not rightly related to God? Can you be saved and not in a right relationship with God? Salvation was taken care of once on Calvary - never to have to been done again. Your salvation has been taken care of if you have asked and sincerely trusted Jesus Christ to be your Lord and Savior. It is possible to be saved and have times when your relationship with God is not right. It is possible to be saved, but out of fellowship temporarily. There are things one needs to do to continue building the relationship. Namely, spend time with God.

How do you develop a close relationship with anybody? You spend time together. Just because you spend time with God, it doesn't necessarily mean every area of your life is going to be perfect, but it does mean you have the Perfect One directing the areas of life we have entrusted to HIM. The more we walk with HIM, the more we trust HIM. The more we trust HIM, the more (of us) we gladly turn over to HIM.

1) Read and write 1st Peter 5:6-7.

Humble yourselves and cast all your care upon Him for He cares for you! Wow! What a soothing thought! He cares for me! Does God care about this? Yes - most definitely. I have heard people say "I don't want to bother God with this or that!" This verse is telling us that He wants to be bothered! He wants to lift us up in due time. If you read further in verse 10, you will see that He wants to perfect, establish, strengthen, and settle us!

I told you on day one that as I lay prostrate on the floor, I cried out to God and totally surrendered my marriage to Him. I could not take it anymore and what's more, I didn't want it. I was exhausted mentally, physically, emotionally, and spiritually. Wiped out you might say. Without knowing what I was doing, I humbled myself before the Almighty, and cast all my care on Him - because I was hoping that He cared for me!

When we decided divorce wasn't an option, we began living in a miserable existence. A short reprieve came as we were blessed with a wonderful, beautiful, blue eyed, blonde haired, baby boy. As soon as life got "back to normal" we were miserable again.

You know, when you hurt, you look for a remedy. I was hurting and I needed a remedy. That's when I started talking to God about marriage. I didn't know much about marriage according to God, but I found it hard to believe He wanted us to have this miserable existence just for the sake of not divorcing. I was right. Marriage is much more than just not divorcing. It is much more than staying together for the sake of the children. It is a relationship like none other. It is the marital relationship that offers us every opportunity to apply all of the principles that God's Word teaches us about how to treat each other. It is the marital relationship that offers the best training for us to learn forgiveness, grace, kindness, tenderness, courtesy, brotherly love, respect, living with one another in understanding, patience, long-suffering, how to think no evil, bear all, endure all, believe all, not behave rudely, and love one another. It is the relationship that is to mirror Christ's love for the church and the churches love for Christ.

It is so much bigger than the two people in it. It is a marriage ordained by God Almighty to bring honor and glory to HIMSELF. It's not just about happiness, it is about holiness. It's not just about pleasure, it is about purpose. It is not something we only pretend to be when the world can see us. It is something we first get right at home. It is something we work on with our spouses and God. He has to lead the way. He has to teach us. We must strive to be blameless before our spouse and God. When we get it right at home, we have it right. When we can stand blameless before our spouse, we are making progress.

Can you imagine how church would be, if our homes were right? Can you imagine how our communities would be if our churches were healthy? Can you imagine how healthy our nation would be if our communities were healthy? Do you see how important our marriages are to God? Do you see how important our marriages are to the next generations? God took us on an incredible journey. We are still on it. God took our marriage and turned it into something He could use for His glory. As long as we are obedient to Him, He can use us. If we are not obedient, and there are times when we do falter, He will not use us.

When a marriage is what it should be, the home is so blessed. The children benefit beyond measure and so does society. When children grow up in the security of knowing mom and dad love each other because they love God and are properly aligned with HIM, we raise a generation that can be productive because they do not have to spend their adult lives sorting through the garbage they had to bring with them into adulthood. God warns us in HIS Word not to deal treacherously with one another. Proper conduct and treatment towards others includes our spouses and children. God has much to say about how we treat our spouses. Can you see how all of this works together?

2) Read Malachi 2:14-16.

    a) Does God care about any of this? What does He say in verse 14?

    b) A husband and wife have a covenant relationship. God has a covenant relationship with His people. He takes the covenant relationships very seriously and expects us to do the same. He makes them one, husband and wife. Why one? (vs. 15)

3) Why do you think God seeks Godly offspring?

    Can you imagine the witness of a generation of Godly offspring?
    I wonder what that world would look like?

4) a) Why does God hate divorce?

    b) What does divorce do? (vs. 16)

5) What do you think "covers one's garment with violence" means?

6) Can you think of a divorced couple and an example that would fit that "violence" description? Explain your answer.

7) How does God warn one to avoid divorce? (vs. 16)

8) If God warns against dealing treacherously with the wife of "your youth" do you think the same applies for dealing treacherously with the husband of your youth? Explain your answer.

Does God care about how you feel? You better believe He does. We don't grow up learning this. I grew up in church. I didn't grow up learning how to have a relationship with God at home or in church. Most people I know that grew up in church say the same thing. How could this not be taught? How can you grow up in a Christian home, (my parents were Christians), and not learn how to have a Christian marriage? How can you grow up in a Christian church and not be taught how to have a relationship with God? I am not sure. Of course there is always the possibility how to develop that relationship was taught in church and I just wasn't paying attention. Ultimately we all have to take responsibility for our individual relationship with God. We learn what we purpose in our hearts to learn. We become familiar with what we spend time with. Sadly, it is our misguided priorities that dictate the state of our relationships, not our faith. The goal of this study is to teach us how to develop a personal relationship with Christ so He can develop our faith and teach us to live accordingly. Spend the remainder of your time today reflecting on what you have learned this week. (Be sure to go back to Day Two and record any improvements you have noticed as a result of making the promise not to speak negatively about your spouse and or marriage for one week.)

WEEK
Three

In the Beginning ... False Images, Part I

Hopefully you are convinced you are not the only one who feels like you do. Years ago I was privileged to speak at a retreat to a group of college/career young, single adults. The theme for their retreat was "a road map for life." We all need a map, a sense of direction, a destination of sorts for this life that we live. I can remember sharing with this group of terrific young people something I heard at a seminar. The speaker said "if you don't know where you are going, you probably won't like where you end up!" Knowing where you are going is a good thing. A map is a good thing to have especially if you don't know where you are going. As I prepared for that retreat, I remember looking at a map and thinking how useless a map is if one doesn't know the starting point. I realize I am really showing my age because maps are pretty much a thing of the past. They have been replaced with GPS devices and internet maps. It is amazing to me that I can put an address in my smartphone, hit a button, and this lady starts giving me directions! Regardless of which method you use for direction, you still need to know your starting point don't you?

Think about it. If you are looking at a map and you see a place you think you might like to go, how would you get there if you didn't know where you were? I remember asking the group, "if I called you on the phone and said I want to come see you, how do I get to your house, what would you ask me?" Of course they answered, we would ask where are you coming from? Can we agree that it is just as crucial to know where you are as it is to know where you are going? Marriage is no different. I can tell you that where I ended up did not remotely resemble where I thought I was going! My marriage didn't look a thing like I imagined it would. My guess is, yours doesn't either. How could it? Does anyone really know what to expect? Where do our preconceptions and misconceptions come from? They come from our beginning! They come from our starting points.

Our starting point comes from all the elements involved in our rearing. When you get to the "I Do's" you not only have your past to contend with, you have your spouse's past to throw into the mix! Take a moment here to think about that. That could be a recipe for disaster. The purpose of this lesson is to take a serious look at where you were before you got to where you are now.

Not long into our marriage, I started realizing things just weren't working out like I thought they were supposed to. I can remember thinking, "wait a minute, I work, clean the house, take care of the pets, cook the meals, wash the clothes, buy the groceries, take care of his mother, take care of my grandmother, and pay the bills. In my mind, all he had to do was go to work. I thought that was a little unbalanced.

We also always seemed to have more month than money - so throw financial struggles into the mix and I was becoming a real bitter woman! What happened to the romance? The candlelit dinners, the romantic evenings out? Where was that emotional comfort and fulfillment I longed for? Where was the excitement for life? It wasn't in our house or marriage! Once I couldn't stand it any longer, we had a talk! I commenced to tell him about all that I did inside and outside of the house, and then I asked "what do you do?" The conversation didn't leave either of us feeling too good about ourselves. You know where we were? We were right smack dab in the middle of REALITY!

This is not how life was supposed to be! Where had we gone wrong? False image, false image, false image! That's what I had about him, that's what he had about me, and that's what we had about marriage! I didn't know that's what was going on. God revealed it to me. I love it when God leads me on a Bible Study. I was studying the Old Testament and it seemed that everything God was revealing to me had to do with false images. I couldn't get away from it. It was false image this, and false image that, and finally one day I asked God, "what is it you are trying to teach me about the false images?" Are you ready for this? THEY AREN'T REAL! FALSE IMAGES ARE THINGS PEOPLE MAKE UP WHEN THEY ARE NOT WALKING WITH GOD AND ARE NOT SEEKING HIS TRUTHS! That's what He taught me.

The Israelites had been rescued from their bondage in Egypt, were on their way to the promised land, and still didn't get it. What did they do? They became impatient when their leader. Moses was gone longer than they thought he should be, so they made their own god, their own false image. Something to worship, bow down to, and give credit to for taking care of them. You know what else I learned? People are people and we are all pretty much alike. When we take our eyes off of God, we are left to our own imaginations. We try to figure out what is best, where it is we should be going, and what it is we need. We build our own false images. We bow down to them. We worship them. Then we get upset when they (our false images) don't perform like we think they should or are supposed to.

Both of us learned we had false images about a lot of things. We had unfairly imagined the other one to be something no man or woman could ever be. We both imagined marriage to be something God never intended it to be. I thought love was a feeling. If I felt good about him, that meant I loved him. If I didn't feel good about him that meant I did not love him anymore! I thought the winner of an argument was the one who could belittle the other one the best. We both thought we should always feel about each other the way we did when we first met. I thought it was his responsibility to make me happy and that should be his primary purpose in life. Can you see how distorted our thinking was? So what did we do about it? How did we figure out what was real and what was false? God took us back to the beginning! That is where we are going to ask you to go. The destination is a God honoring marriage. We need to know how to get there, but first we are going to figure out where we are coming from.

The next two weeks are just for you. The daily work is designed to give insight about you! It is perhaps the first time you will have given thought to who you were before you were married, why you were that way, and, in next week's lesson, who you are now and why you are like you are. To some, it might not sound like an exciting venture, but please do not skip this very important part of the study. I will disclose that you will come across some questions that, depending on your background and how you were raised, might not leave you feeling too good. While it is not the intent to make you feel bad, I firmly believe we must face the truth about where we are and how we got here before we can understand the importance of seeking, learning, and living out God's Truths.

We are all raised a particular way - and we have no choice in the hand that was dealt us as children. We did not pick the families we were born into and we had no say so in who raised us or how we were raised. The people involved in our childhood, in essence, mold us into who we become by the age of eighteen. We are susceptible to their influences and ideals. The sum of who they are, make up who we are. Here is the key. If we were not raised with an understanding of who we were created to be, if we were not raised with the knowledge of whose image we were created in, we have problems! I grew up in what I knew to be a Christian home. I grew up in church. I learned a lot of wonderful Bible stories, and heard a lot of great sermons I am sure however, I did not grow up learning who I was created to be. Implied maybe, but emphasis on being created in God's image, emphasis on His plan, His Kingdom, walking in His Word verses the world? NO! I did not grow up learning that. Nor did I grow up learning what marriage, according to God, was supposed to be. I do not blame my parents for that. They were wonderful people. I believe they were like most of us. If we are not actively and intentionally seeking God and His ways, we are automatically being transformed in the ways of the world. Romans 12:2

instructs us to not be conformed to this world but to be transformed by the renewing of your mind that you may prove what that good and acceptable and perfect will of God is. I am grateful my parents raised me and my brothers in church though because I caught enough of the truth to know where to turn when my life was totally out of hand!

Neither do I blame the pastors or the Sunday school teachers I had. I am sure they taught exactly what I needed to learn, and perhaps I missed it. Whether I learned what I needed to or not, I believe church was the best place for me to be raised. It made me aware of God and Jesus. I believe going to church properly tilled the soil of my heart so that when the seed (word of God) did fall on my heart, it took root! Parents, take your children to church! The truth is, we can be in the right place and hear all of the right things and totally ignore the truth. We have to take personal responsibility for our own personal relationship with God. God's plan for marriage and raising children is revealed in HIS WORD. His ways are not our ways and His thoughts are not our thoughts. His world is different than ours. His world is where we want to go. Thy Kingdom come, Thy Will be done on EARTH as it is in Heaven. He wants us to look like the image we were created in. He wants our marriages to look like He created them to look. He wants our children to know the security of growing up in a home where mom and dad are one. There is not a safer more productive environment for a child to grow in. It eliminates a lot of garbage they would otherwise have to carry into their adulthood. It would have eliminated a lot of the garbage you had to carry with you into your adulthood. When I think of the many hours it has taken me to learn all of that, in my own quiet time alone with Him seeking His Truths, I am grateful to my parents, my pastors, and my Sunday School teachers for pointing me in the right direction. The next two lessons are going to point you in that same direction. It is designed to help you sort out what you need to hold on to or get rid of. Over the next two weeks, you are going to have a lot of things revealed to you about yourself.

WARNING!!! It is not for the faint at heart. There may be areas you just cannot visit at this time. That is okay. This course is designed to take over and over, again and again. I have not only taken this course myself a gazillion times, I have gone back to it many times in between classes! Every time I do that, I have more things revealed to me and more questions answered. It is a journey to a promised land. We can assure you that you will not be sorry if you go on this trip. But just like we talked on page one, you need a map (or a GPS!). You need to know where your starting point is. This is your starting point. YOU ARE HERE! Please take your time answering the questions. If you come across one you just don't want to tackle right now, great! Leave it for another time. You will be so glad you went on this journey. If you will take this seriously, we can promise your family will benefit beyond your greatest expectations. Grab a cup of coffee or tea and enjoy the journey. Just like the Israelites, you are about to be set free!

Day One – What were you like before you got married?

Can you remember back that far? For some it might be less than two years. For others, it might be 20 + years. Whatever your situation, you still remember what you were like before you got married. It seems to be something we never forget. Before you got married, you had an image of yourself, your spouse, and marriage. Webster's defines image as: a mental picture of something absent or to picture in mind or imagine; Imaginary: existing only in the imagination; and imagine: to form a mental picture of; to suppose; to think of. Those definitions are familiar to all of us. We all know what it is like to have an image of something and to visit our own imaginations. In fact, it is safe to say we can actually live our lives according to imagery, mental pictures that have nothing to do with the way things really are. I do not know anyone personally that grew up with a real knowledge of who they were created to be in Christ. I know a lot of people that grew up in Christian homes and went to church. I do not know anyone, personally, that grew up walking with Jesus Christ daily, not so I could tell anyway! That doesn't mean there weren't people around me who had that daily walk. It means, if they were, I missed it. That says a lot more about me and the world's influence on me, than it does them if there were people like that in my life. I am happy to say I do know people today that walk with Him daily.

What is so sad about that is how we become what we become based on false information. Our marriages become what they become based on false information. Let me give you some examples. Let's say you grew up in a house where you were made fun of or told you were stupid. It could have been a parent or sibling that told you those things. I am not just talking about an occasional situation. I mean you were told that all the time. By the time you went to school, you thought you were stupid! Because your parent or parents thought that of you, you believed that about yourself. Now, in a different environment, you are being made fun of by the other students. Perhaps your teacher thinks the same thing. So far, you have been in two environments in your brief lifetime, home and school, and in both environments, this negative image is being built in your mind. No one has bothered to tell you that you were fearfully and wonderfully made, and that you were created in His image. All you know is you have been made fun of your whole, albeit short, life. You start thinking that about yourself and now, without your knowledge, you are doomed to a life of inadequacy. It doesn't have to be the word "stupid." Substitute any negative thing in its place. The outcome is the same. Put a positive in its place, you become that. Positive or negative - it doesn't matter. Was it of God? If what you grew up thinking about yourself was not of God, or a reflection of HIS image, it was a false image and you have some "truth finding and overcoming" to do. Chances are, so does your spouse. We are going to take a look at those "formative" influences and the environments that molded us. We will see how much of it we need to hang onto. Ready?

1) Do you remember what your life was like before you got married? Describe it.

2) Where were you living when you met your spouse?

3) What kind of responsibilities did you have before you met your spouse ?

4) Describe your personality when you met your spouse.

5) Were you a Christian before you got married? And what did being a Christian mean?

6) What type of social activities did you like to participate in?

7) a) How would you describe your relationship with your parents while you were growing up?

   b) Did the relationship change when you grew up and either moved out on your own, or by the time you met your spouse-to-be?

8) Did you have many friends growing up? Describe those friendships.

9) Who in your family or circle of friends (including your friends families and parents) had the most positive influence on you and why?

Answer the same question with regards to the most negative influence on you and why.

10) a) What types of things made you happy before you got married?

   b) Sad?

   c) Angry?

   d) Describe your actions when you were experiencing those emotions.

Read Psalm 94:11-12, 19. Spend the remainder of your time this morning writing in your journal about anything you can remember about your life and what you were like before you met your spouse and got married. Even if it feels silly, write about anything that comes to mind. Give particular attention to how much of a role God played in your life prior to meeting your spouse. What were your "religious" beliefs? How much time did you spend in church? How much time did you spend reading your Bible? How much time did you spend in prayer alone and with other people? Describe your relationship (or lack thereof) with God.

Day Two – Do you know why you were that way?

Yesterday you devoted time to remembering what your life was like prior to getting married. You answered questions and hopefully thought of some other things from your past that helped you recall what you were like before you got married. Today we are going to focus on knowing why you were like you were and how that may have influenced your relationship with your spouse.

1) Lets start by taking a look at the relationship. How did you meet your spouse?

2) a) What attracted you to each other?

   b) What made him/her the right one?

   c) What was your idea of a "man / woman" and where do you think that idea came from? Did you think your "spouse to be" met the ideals you had of a man/woman?

3) Where was your spouse living when you started dating? What were his/her responsibilities?

4) a) What type of things did you do while dating?

b) What was your idea of romance?

c) What was your spouse's idea of romance?

d) Was your dating life romantic?

e) Did you have pre-marital sex?

f) What were your beliefs about pre-marital sex and where did you get those beliefs from?

5) Was your "spouse to be" a Christian and what did being a Christian mean to him/her?

6) Was Christianity or church a part of your dating life? Explain.

7) How did you become engaged?

8) a) Prior to becoming engaged, did you ever discuss things like finances, children, beliefs, responsibilities, Christianity, etc.?

   b) What specifically do you remember about these issues and were you like-minded?

9) a) Did you, as a couple, have a large circle of friends?

   b) If so, did you see your friends often and how did you spend your time together with them?

10) Describe the relationship you had with your spouse when you were dating. (Was it fun, exciting, boring, did you love him/her, did you like him/her, how did he/she make you feel, how did you make him/her feel? Did you argue? If so, how much?)

11) Now that you have given thought to what you were like before you got married, and now that you have revisited the "dating" years, try to put into words why you think you were like you were. (For instance, I was happy, in love, and didn't know the first thing about what it took to live on my own in the real world. That is why I was like I was. I had been taken care of all my life. I had no responsibility to speak of. I thought life was fun and games primarily. So did he. What a recipe for disaster! I had started a walk with Christ but most of my thoughts about life were worldly and self-centered as opposed to God-centered)

We read Psalm 1 last week. Our focus was on the counsel you seek, who you talk to, and what type of influence you are under. Now I want you to meditate on this Psalm again. Spend the remainder of your time this morning writing in your journal about how your life (as you were growing up and before you were married) and this Psalm compare.

Day Three – Did you change?

This has been a walk down memory lane, huh? You have looked at what you were like growing up. You know what you were like when you met your spouse-to-be. You know what the relationship was like, and why you think all of that was. Today we want to spend time looking at the changes, if any, that have taken place.

1) Do you remember what your image of your spouse was when you met? (This is before you really got to know him/her - what did you imagine him/her to be?) When you answer this question, I want you to think about your spouse in terms of what you either imagined him/her to be, or hoped he/she was. Then, honestly answer this question: is your spouse what you imagined him/her to be?

2) Do you think you fell in love with the person or the image you had of them? Explain.

3) My guess is, you fell in love with something you had hoped he/she was, only to find out they might not have lived up to the image. In all fairness, and giving the benefit of the doubt, let's say your spouse wasn't too far off the mark. As masks and veils have come off through the years, as flaws have been revealed, would you say your spouse changed, or would you say the image of what you thought they should be has changed?

Are you starting to have some things revealed to you? Somewhere along the way, one or both of you changed. Please know that is **VERY NORMAL!** We cannot stay the same forever. Our circumstances change. The wind blows, the rains come, and floods happen. Life events require us to change. We could not possibly know at age 25 and single what we know at age 35, married, with a mortgage, and 3 children. Change is very common. It does not mean that a marriage has to end because one or both of you have changed in some way. It means you have been promoted to a new position in life. New responsibilities come with promotions. Liken it to a promotion at work. If you flip hamburgers and get promoted to manager, do you continue flipping the hamburgers? You might have to flip a burger every once in a while, but that is not your primary responsibility any longer. If you do not learn how to handle your new responsibilities, you will fail and likely be fired. The establishment you are supposed to be running will crumble and fall too. That is what happens to our marriages and families when we do not grow with our promotions and responsibilities. They crumble and fall. We will talk more about promotions in another chapter. You have had an opportunity the last couple of days to review who you were, (as well as you can remember), and why you think you were that way. Now, I want you to give thought to how you have changed and reflect on why you have changed. Here are some questions to help you get started.

4) a) Do you have any resentment towards your spouse?

    b) If so, why?

    c) Why didn't you have that resentment when you were dating and first married?

5) a) Do you and your spouse have as much in common now as you did when you were dating?

    b) Describe the things you had in common when you dated and list the things you have in common now.

6) a) Do you have children?

    b) If so, are you both equally involved in raising them (in terms of meeting all their needs spiritually, physically, mentally, emotionally, socially, etc.).

    c) Describe the relationship / family dynamics in terms of how the children have changed your relationship. (Basically, what is the family life like inside your home?)

Do you see where I am going with this? Your life events change, why wouldn't you? Of course your relationship has changed. The natural course of life introduces us to new and different seasons that require change. Most of us not only resist change, we fail miserably at it! We are not taught in school (or anywhere else in the world) how to prepare for the changes. In the Christian world, we are supposed to be taught by the older men and women according to Titus 2: 3-5. How many of you have been? It is all there in the Bible. So why do we get to this stage in our lives (whatever stage you are) and still not have this figured out?

I can tell you how and why most people change. We allow resentment to build up because, A) our spouse doesn't live life the way we think they should, B) often our spouse has not become what we think they should or hoped they would, and C) our needs are no longer being met by our spouse. As the years have passed you have grown farther apart and have very little in common anymore (if anything). Let's not forget about the children. Children add a whole new dimension to the relationship. There have been different ideas on how to raise them, or one of you has primarily raised them alone. There is a huge divide in your relationship because of that. The "divide" has been one you have learned to live with. Neither of you have any idea how to mend that gap. Am I anywhere close to describing your situation? Spend the remainder of your time this morning writing in your journal final thoughts about what, if anything, you are beginning to understand about yourself and/or the relationship. Read Psalm 100: 3-5. Reflect on those scriptures the rest of the day!

Day Four – What was your spouse like before he/she was your spouse?

How are you doing so far? If this has been difficult for you, be of good cheer. You are in great company. I spoke with a friend the other day who has taken this course three times and she admitted to me that she never could completely go through the "image" study because it was too difficult for her. I know this can be painful at times. Perhaps your childhood was not so good. Maybe these questions bring up bad memories. Perhaps your life is in a painful season right now and these questions (or your answers) are causing you to feel like you have made some mistakes. Please, hear me out. All of us have those feelings. You are not alone in this walk. Which one of us has done "life" perfectly? There is only one who lived perfectly. His name is Jesus. He is God. We are not HIM! I am offering some encouragement here because we have further to go. It is so important to know where you are starting from. Remember the map?

Jesus had one purpose. He came to do His Father's will. He did it. I didn't grow up understanding my purpose. Did you? Can you imagine how different our lives would be if we not only grew up knowing who we were created to be in Christ Jesus, but we understood our sole purpose was to do our Heavenly Fathers will? Life would be a bit different wouldn't it if we all lived God's will as it pertains to marriage? We can't change our spouses to be what God has called them to be, but we can understand what the roles looks like.

I learned what the husband's role looked like, by seeking my role as a wife. That is what this course will give you the opportunity to do, seek your role as a Christian husband / wife. You might be tempted to shift the focus from who you are supposed to become so you can spend time working on your spouse! I am going to encourage you to just focus on you. As important as it was for you to understand some things about yourself prior to getting married, it is equally important to understand some things about your spouse before they became your spouse. When I allowed myself to do this exercise, my heart started to want to soften towards my husband. I started to realize he was just as disadvantaged about the things of marriage as I was. He was just as uninformed about who he was supposed to be in Christ as I was. I started to understand we were two impaired people that wanted to love one another. We, at least at one time, wanted to treat each other right and be what we were supposed to be. My heart started to change once I realized we were both in the same boat. That, my friend, was when God started teaching me compassion, not only for my husband, but for myself and all of humanity.

I know this "false image" stuff is difficult, but please go through it and let the Holy Spirit reveal the things to you that are going to set you free. Knowing the truth and living by it sets us free. Today we are going to concentrate on what your spouse was like before you got married.

In previous exercises, you have given thought to some of these questions. If you feel like you have already answered some of them in enough detail, move onto the next one.

1) I know you have already answered where your spouse was living when you met, and what their responsibilities were, so if you feel like you have exhausted your knowledge of those responsibilities, go onto the next question, if not, please spend more time on your recollection of where he/she was living and what their responsibilities were prior to meeting and getting married.

2) Describe his/her personality when you met.

3)   What type of things (hobbies, interest, etc.) did he/she like when you met?

4)   What was his/her home life/family life like?

5)   Who had a positive influence on their childhood and what made it a positive influence?

     Who had a negative influence and what made it negative?

6)   What was his/her concept of marriage?

7)   Did (or do) his/her parents have a good marriage?
     Describe their marriage.

8) Did he/she have any heroes or idols? Who were they and what made them a hero/idol?

9) I know you have already answered the question if he/she was a Christian, but please revisit the question and write your thoughts about what his/her beliefs were at the time you met.

10) Did he/she have a lot of friends? Was he/she very socially active? What types of things did he/she do and how were they viewed by their peers?

11) What made him/her happy? Sad? Angry? etc. and how were those emotions acted out?

12) What were their ideas/beliefs on the role of a husband? A wife?

Your attitude towards your spouse at this very moment probably influenced your answers. Your attitude could be different tomorrow or next week. If you were not particularly kind towards your spouse in answering some of these questions, please do yourself a favor and revisit this section in the future. It might offer more insight into who they were when you met, which could explain a lot of things about who they are now! The good thing about this course is it can be taken over and over and over again. Each time you can learn new things about your situation. Hopefully you had some things revealed to you about your spouse that allowed you, like it did me, to start having compassion.

When I started this journey, things were so bad between us I didn't know where to begin. As God started revealing compassion to me, I wasn't ready to call a truce just yet, but it allowed me to at least realize he was deserving of a display of kindness from me. If I could show a complete stranger acts of kindness, God let me know I needed to treat my husband with kindness too. It didn't matter if I thought he deserved it or not. That was just an opinion based on how I felt at any given moment anyway. I am commanded as a Christian to treat others with kindness. That means my husband too! Spend the remainder of your time this morning writing thoughts (of kindness) towards your spouse with regards to what his/her life may have been like before you got married. Give thought to how his/her life could have been better. Read 1st Peter 3:8-12 and let your meditation with our Lord reveal the blessing you are called to be to your spouse.

Day Five – What was your image of marriage before you got married?

I know this has probably been a "mixed emotions" type of week for you. Aren't you glad day five is here? This can be a fun day, or it can be one of those "how could I have been so naïve" days, depending on the answers to these questions. The good news is we all probably had the same image of marriage before we got married. Therefore, we were all in the same boat! Your image of marriage very likely came from two sources. One, your interpretation of your parent's marriage, and two, your thoughts on what your marriage was going to be like. The thoughts of what your marriage was going to be like were a culmination of several different influences, i.e. movies, love stories, daydreams, other family member or friends parents, etc.

1) Describe your parents' marriage as well as you can remember it.

2) a) What did you like about their marriage?

   b) What did you dislike about it?

3) a) Who did you know that had a good marriage?

   b) What made their marriage good?

   c) Are they still together today?

   d) What are your thoughts on their marriage today?

4) a) Who did you know that had a bad marriage?

    b) What made that marriage bad?

    c) Are they still together today?

    d) What are your thoughts on their marriage today?

5) In thinking about the "good marriage" vs. "bad marriage" scenarios above, describe how well you knew those couples, i.e. how much time did you spend in their homes, what was your relationship with them, how much did you know about their personal lives?

6) How was your marriage going to be like and different than the marriages you have described?

7) Has your marriage lived up to the image you had of it? Why do you think it has or has not?

8) How has your marriage resembled the marriages you have described? Why do you think it has or has not?

We will talk more next week about our images of marriage and how they have changed. I want to congratulate you on finishing this lesson! I know it can be difficult to look back at the things I have asked you to consider this week. The good news is, your "starting point" should be coming into view by now. I want to end this lesson by doing something a little different. Spend the remainder of your time this morning by pouring your heart out to God. Let Him know that you know He has seen all of your answers. Confess whatever you might need to confess if you do not feel good about something. Ask Him to start preparing your heart for His Truths about marriage and the relationship He wants you to have with your spouse. Let me encourage you to write about the thoughts that are on your heart right now, about where you are, and where you hope to go. Read Psalm 139:23-24. Record whatever you sense God might be revealing to you.

WEEK
Four

When the honeymoon is over ... False Images, Part II

This week we are going to take a look at where you are now. It will be good to take a good honest look at what you are like now, why you are like you are, how your image of marriage has changed, and how your spouse has changed. We will also give consideration to whether your marriage is A) irritable, B) irreparable, or C) irreplaceable.

I can remember thinking our honeymoon would never end. I would always hear married couples talking about the honeymoon being over, but I wrote that off as them never really being in love. The honeymoon was not an event in my mind it was a description of the marriage. I just knew we were going to be in love and flying high emotionally forever! I was so wrong! I can almost pinpoint the exact moment our honeymoon was over. After we celebrated our first anniversary, things started to change. Our first year of marriage was a piece of cake! For most people, it is the hardest, and I understand that. We talked about that in our first lesson. For us, however, it was the easiest.

My mother died with pancreatic cancer three days after we got married. Her illness was the most important thing on my mind as we were getting married. Within a month after we were married, I had my gallbladder removed. That was major surgery in the 80's! To complicate matters, I spent a week in the hospital with a staph infection. My recovery did not go as planned. It was at least six weeks before I was back to normal. Shortly after that, I lost my job. Shortly after that, Ray lost his. We were so bombarded in our first year with tragedy we gladly clung to each other. We were all we had! As we grieved the death of my mother, made it past the surgery and the job losses, and began to get our feet back on the ground, we started to settle into life.

All of a sudden, life wasn't fun anymore. The thrill of seeing our cars parked side by side in the driveway and ironing his shirts just didn't seem to have the same sentiment they once had. I felt like most of the responsibility was falling on me and I was getting pretty angry about it. Playing house was not at all what I imagined it would be. Breakfast in bed stopped and we both could tell the honeymoon was over! Love was slowly being replaced by resentment and the relationship we once had, was quickly fading away. We were now having to put effort into a relationship that was, at one time, effortless. It was during this time that a friend invited us to go to church with her and her husband. We didn't know it then, but that would prove to be a key part to our marriage being saved. That is where we met the preacher we counseled with.

When the honeymoon is over, the work begins. Can you remember when your honeymoon was over? It usually ends as soon as the responsibilities of life seep into the marriage. Those responsibilities are usually not present when you are dating. For a few dating hours, you get to leave your responsibilities behind. Dating is kind of a fun "time out" from real life. We trick ourselves into thinking life could always be "this" way, with "this" person. So we get married. We have a honeymoon stage. For a while, things couldn't be better. Then the responsibilities of life find us and start destroying our happy little false image world. Resentment builds on both sides. Before we know it, we are not just out of love we are out of like. We start dealing treacherously with each other (which we will talk more about in coming weeks). All of the sudden we don't even resemble ourselves.

If you can relate, hopefully you will find some comfort in knowing you are not alone. Also, let me encourage you by saying once the honeymoon is over, and you understand it is inevitable and normal, you can start building your marriage on truth. You can let go of the false images you may have entered the marriage with. You have a better understanding, after last week, of what you both were like before you got married and why you were that way. This week we are going to concentrate on what you both have become and how you got from where you were to where you are.

The purpose of all of this is to discover what you are really dealing with. Is your life/marriage based on imagery, false images, or truth? Sadly, I find it doesn't matter if you are a Christian or not. I know it should and that is a message we believe God wants us to share. I hear men and women say "how could I be a Christian and feel this way about my spouse?" My answer is "easy!" We are not taught in the Christian world what a Christian marriage, wife, or husband is supposed to be. We go to church, we treat others with Christian love and brotherly kindness, get in the car and either fight with or ignore each other Sunday from 12:00 noon until the following Sunday just before we walk into Sunday School. We know something is not right because we are Christians and we certainly shouldn't feel this way about our spouses. It is devastating to us that we do feel this way. It is such a burden, we feel guilty even sharing it with anyone. In many cases, we don't share it. We learn to live with it and we are absolutely miserable. The world tells us we married the wrong person. The world's answer is to divorce and go find someone we can be happy with. The children will understand. They are resilient. We fool ourselves into believing that living with another man and /or allowing our children to have another mother won't mess them up. Here is some truth: It does mess the children up. They do not understand it! Obtaining another husband, wife, house, car, boat, child **WILL NOT FIX IT!!!** What will not mess the children up and what they will understand is a mom and dad that surrender themselves and their marriage to God. God's Word tells us divorce covers everybody's garment with violence (Malachi 2:16). The truth is, we can't fix it. God can!

We need to seek Him in our roles and ideals for marriage. Our churches might offer classes that set us on the right path to learning how to have Christian marriages and homes, but we cannot expect the church to accept the full responsibility of fixing our messed up marriages, any more than we can expect the church to accept the full responsibility of raising our children. We must accept responsibility for our marriages and raising our children. Our personal search and obedience to God's word is how Christians become Christian wives, Christian husbands, and have Christian marriages. After this week, you will know exactly where you are. That is a great place to be. I am excited for you because once this part of the course is over you can start comparing your false images to God's truths. When you see what you have and why you have it (false images), contrasted with what God wants to give you and why He wants you to have it (God's Truth), you are going to wonder, just like I did, why has it taken me so long to seek HIM in this???? Ready?

Day One - What are you like now?

1) How would you describe yourself spiritually, mentally, and physically?

2) Considering your answer above, what would you say is the biggest change in you since getting married?

3) Why do you think that change has come about?

4) How has that change affected your marriage?

5) Would you say the honeymoon is over? If so, when did it end? What was the "honeymoon" supposed to be like and how long was it supposed to last?

Read Psalm 31:1. Spend the rest of your time this morning meditating on that verse. There are 3 short sentences (if you are reading the New King James Version). "In you Oh Lord, I put my Trust. Let me never be ashamed. Deliver me in Your righteousness."

In relation to your marriage what do you think it means to: 1) put your trust in the Lord, 2) never be ashamed, and 3) be delivered in His righteousness? Record your thoughts in your journal.

Tomorrow we are going to look at why we are like we are now.

Day Two - Self Examination - Why are you like you are now?

It can be painful to put yourself through an honest self-examination can't it? Have you ever really done that? It is not hard to examine your spouse's life and tell him/her how to improve. To examine yourself for strengths and weaknesses is a tough thing to do. The strengths might not present the problem, but how about the weaknesses? Who has time to think about those? After all, just going through our day and handling all of our responsibilities takes up all of our time. Who has time to ponder a weakness? According to the Bible, we all should!

1)   Read Psalm 139:23-24. Write those verses:

2)   What did the Psalmist ask God to do?

3)   What does it mean to ask God to search you?

4)   What does it mean to ask God to "know your heart?"

5)   What does it mean to ask God to "try you and know your anxieties?"

6) Has God ever shown you any "wicked" way in you and led you in another direction, in His everlasting way? Explain what that means to you.

Spend the remainder of your time today asking God to search your heart and reveal to you whatever He would about who you are, what your anxieties are, what, if any, are the wicked ways in your heart. Then ask Him to show you a glimpse of what His leading in your life could produce. I have given you some questions to help with this process. Let me encourage you to write about anything that comes to mind.

1) Describe the person you believe yourself to be right now.

2) Ask God to look into your heart right now and whisper the things He sees: (Good or bad, make a list of whatever comes to mind after praying that prayer.)

3) List any anxieties you might be having in your life right now. Is there anything with your spouse that is causing you to be anxious? Your children? Job? Money? Other relationships?

4) Emotionally, how are you handling the things you have described above? For instance, are you short tempered because of the anxiety in your life?

5) What is in your life right now that makes you happy? How do you express your happiness?

6) What is in your life right now making you sad? How do you express your sadness?

7) What is in your life right now making you angry? How do you express your anger?

8) What is in your life right now making you content? How do you express that contentment?

9) Do any of those things affect your relationship with your spouse? If so how? If not, why not?

10) Do you like the person you have become? Why or why not?

Day Three - Has your image of marriage changed?

My image of marriage has definitely changed. As I have already shared, in our second year I started suspecting this marriage thing wasn't at all what I had imagined it to be. If there was ever any doubt, what I am about to share, really did the trick! We had been married for three, maybe four, years. In addition to taking care of things around our house, I was the primary care giver for my grandmother. Ray's mother was not in good health, so I did what I could to help her as well. One Saturday I had been to my grandmothers to clean her house and go to the grocery store for her. I then went and did the same for my mother-in-law. It was late afternoon and I was finally heading home. I still had the cleaning and grocery store chore for us facing me when I got home. For some strange reason, I started to imagine that Ray was going to have our house clean and the groceries bought when I got home as a way to thank me for taking care of his mother. After all, marriage was a partnership, right? I imagined he had the house sparkling and dinner in the oven! Or better yet, maybe he was going to have the house sparkling, the groceries put away, and he was taking me out for the evening! I was so in love with him by the time I got home I didn't know what to do!

You can imagine the shock on my face when I walked in the door and saw him sitting on the sofa watching television. The laundry had not been touched. The house was as big a wreck upon my return as it was when I left. The grocery shopping was still waiting for me to do. Nothing that remotely resembled dinner was anywhere around! So much for that wonderful ride home! Forget being in love with him! I didn't speak to him for weeks! You want to know the sad part? I was angry over something I had made up in my own mind! He didn't have any idea I had conjured up that pretty little picture in my mind! I blew a gasket! My hope that things would change without us having to work at it was gone. My image of what I thought marriage should be was shattered, and I didn't like the "real deal."

1) What did you think your marriage was going to be like?

2) Has that image changed? If so. how? If not, why do you think it has not?

3) Do you know couples that seem to have "it" all together? If so, describe what you think their marriage is like and what it is they have that you would like to have in your marriage?

4) In an earlier lesson you described the ideal marriage. Now that we have had some other things in this course to think about, describe how you think your marriage could improve.

5) What do you think you could do to help your marriage more closely resemble the ideal marriage you described?

Hopefully you realize most people experience basically the same things in marriage. You are not alone. You had false images going into the marriage and now truths are being revealed. It doesn't mean you are helpless, or your marriage is hopeless. It means you are just like everybody else and you have a decision to make. Are you going to divorce? Will you stay together and live miserably the rest of your lives? Or are you going to try it God's way?

Spend the remainder of the time talking to God about those choices. Earnestly seek Him in prayer and ask Him to reveal any false images you might still be clinging to. Ask Him to give you a fresh clean slate, mentally, so you can begin to see marriage as it really should be according to Him. Try to erase what you thought it should be or would be. Let me also encourage you not to worry about how you or your spouse might need to change. God will reveal that in time. All you need to concentrate on right now is developing a true image of what marriage is supposed to be. Read Colossians 3:1-17. Ask God to reveal how applying those principles in your home would affect your marriage and home life?

Day Four – Has your spouse changed?

This is going to be a short section because I don't want to give us the opportunity to complain about our spouse. In the most honest, and least negative way that you can, I want you to think about how well you know your spouse. I know we have answered these questions at various places in this study so far, but I want you to answer these questions back to back on this page so you can have the answers in one place.

1) What was your spouse like (personality wise) when you met?

2) What attracted you to your spouse?

3) Where did you go and what did you do on dates?

4) Do you still date? If so, where do you go and what do you do on dates now? If not, why not?

5) What attracted your husband/wife to you?

6) Were those attractions real or false images?

7) Do those attractions still exist today? Why or why not? Are those things still important?

8) What was your spouse's image of marriage before you were married?

9) Has it changed? If so how? If not, why not?

Read Colossians 3:23-25. Spend the remainder of your time in this study today writing about the personal responsibility we all have to God. Concentrate on the truth of those scriptures with regards to being accountable for your own actions. Pray for your spouse. Pray with your spouse.

Day Five – Is your marriage irritable, irreparable, or irreplaceable?

Isn't that an odd question? What do I mean by irritable, irreparable, or irreplaceable? We have learned that most people are very much alike. If your study to this point has you relating to what has been said, it is a good chance your marriage is irritable. An irreparable marriage, in my opinion, is one where abusive behavior is or has been a continual threat to the mental or physical safety of the family members. I would not encourage anybody to stay in an unsafe environment. That type of situation is not addressed in this course. I would encourage anyone dealing with that to seek safety first, and then professional help. While God is perfectly capable of healing anyone and any marriage, that situation calls for much more than I know. That situation needs to be dealt with before the marriage can be addressed.

Unlike an abusive environment, a marriage faced with infidelity, in my opinion, does not necessarily have to be irreparable. If the infidelity is an act clearly ended, repentance is sought and forgiveness granted, the marriage can be salvaged. If, however, the infidelity is a lifestyle the marriage is irreparable in my opinion. The irreplaceable marriage is the one that brings honor to God. Husband and wife honor God and each other. The family is secure in God's will. That is the one that God builds. Does it take the husband and wife to make that decision before it will happen? Let's explore that question.

1) Which of the above best describes your marriage? Why?

2) Hopefully you wrote irreplaceable, but just in case you didn't, if you wrote irritable, write what you think it is going to take to move from the irritable to the irreplaceable. (If you wrote irreparable, feel free to continue with this course. I strongly advise you to seek help aside from this course. Please seek professional help and remove yourself and your children if you feel you are in a dangerous situation.)

Did your answer above indicate that you or your spouse had the biggest changes to make? Let me be as lovingly honest here as I possibly can be. Do yourself a favor right now and forget about the changes your spouse needs to make. Just dismiss them from your mind. I am not saying the changes he/she has to make are not important, because they are. Neither am I suggesting he/she doesn't have to change. I am merely telling you, from experience, you cannot now, have not in the past, and will not in the future, change him/her. This is where I am going to ask you to leave your spouse's faults behind, mentally, for a while, as you go through the rest of this course. There will be a few more questions in later sections that will ask you to describe what your spouse might think of a particular subject, but for the most part, the rest of the study will focus on you and God's truths. I know you are tempted to think that if "he or she" would just (fill in the blank), then everything would be okay. The truth is, that is not the truth.

We will not be held accountable for what our spouse does or does not become. Neither will they be held accountable for what we do or do not become. Each of us will stand before our maker one day and give an account of what we have become. In fact, Jesus says in Matthew 12: 36-37 that "for every idle word men may speak, they will give account of it in the day of judgment. For by your words you will be justified, and by your words you will be condemned." Notice He didn't say, "but you don't have to give an account if your spouse does not do what he/she is supposed to." No, He said we will give an account in the day of judgment and by our words we would be justified or condemned. I don't know about you, but that is incentive for me to keep my eyes off of my spouse's faults and start working on my own!

It was quite a relief to me, Ray, and our marriage when I was convicted to keep my nose out of Ray's and God's relationship and just concentrate on my own relationship with God. I was trying to do everything I thought he should have been doing, plus what I thought I was supposed to do, all without consulting with God. I am embarrassed to admit it, but as much as I said I wanted him to be the head of the household and the spiritual leader, I dared him to take away my power! I was in charge and I liked it! It just sounded more Christian to say "I wish he would be the leader in the home." While I was self- righteously looking at him and his faults, there is no telling what God was thinking about me. Actually, there was a lot God was thinking about me, and He was about to let me know it!

God started showing me I needed to be knowledgeable about my role as a Christian woman, wife, and mother. Knowing what the husband was supposed to be and do was good for me to be able to pray for Ray, but I couldn't make him be those things. I only have control over one person, me. I needed to seek the scriptures to teach me about me and what God created me to be. When I grasped hold of that concept, and was able to leave Ray alone, things started moving from irritable to irreplaceable.

Spend the remainder of your time today telling God how you feel about having to let go of your resentments and desires for your spouse to change. Ask God to search your heart and reveal to you the things He wants you to let go of. Ask Him to reveal to you the things He wants you to concentrate on. Ask Him to give you a picture of what your marriage could look like if you were the only one who changed. Ask for a peace about the changes you need to make. Search scriptures to help you with this. Here are some scriptures to get you started. Proverbs 3:5-6, Psalm 1, 1stCorinthians13. Record your thoughts in your journal.

WEEK
Five

What is the truth?

I love it when the false image study is over! Congrats on making it to week five! We have talked about how we feel. We have talked about how we were in the beginning and how we are now that the honeymoon is over. We have uncovered a lot of the false images that have shaped our lives and influenced who we have become. So what is the truth? How do you find the truth? What makes truth, truth? Will knowing the truth make any difference in my life? Will it make any difference in my marriage? Will it make any difference in my spouse's life? There are lots of questions aren't there? We are going to answer them the best we can and hopefully this study, particularly this section, will make you hungry enough to always seek the truth in all situations and circumstances. When we are dealing with the truth, we can find truthful resolves. When we are not dealing with the truth, we are wasting time and energy.

Do you really want to know the truth? I believe most people do. We get to a point in our lives, good or bad, we are ready to hear the truth aren't we? In fact, the quality of our lives depends on knowing the truth. While perception can be construed as reality, perception is not necessarily the truth. God's Word is the truth. The Word sanctifies us it sets us apart from the world. Our faith should shape our life and lifestyle.

The more we learn about God, the more we learn about His standards for living. It is His standard that we should concern ourselves with, no other standard matters for the Christian. The world is full of self- help instruction. As common sense as some or all of it might be, if it is not a standard God has set, Christians should not be measuring or living our lives by it. I was so happy God loved me enough to show me how I had lived my life according to the world's way. I was even happier to have Him reveal that I didn't have to live like that anymore. I was delighted to learn He had a better way. I asked you last week in Day 5 to forget about the changes your spouse needs to make. I hope you were able to do that. Now, I am going to ask you to forget about the changes you might need to make. I am going to ask you to forget who you have become and how you have gotten here. Let me encourage you right now to clear your mind of any preconceived ideas you have of the man or woman's role in the home, family, and in our culture. Have a blank page in your heart and mind as you answer the questions in this lesson.

Concentrate on the scriptures we will be studying. Ask the Holy Spirit, the spirit of truth to reveal the things to you He would have you learn.

This is my absolute favorite part of the study. In this section, we are going to study the truth to find out what the truth really is. Chains are going to be loosened for you in this lesson. Before we move on, we are going to understand we have a Heavenly Father who created us in His image. We are going to learn we no longer have to live under false images. We will learn we can stop passing on the sins from the generations before us to the generations behind us. And we are going to learn we can stop the sins and enjoy the blessings! So! Where do you find God's truths in the Bible? From Genesis to Revelation! It doesn't matter how many times you read it or in what order. There are always new revelations, new lessons, new insights, new truths. Please treat yourself every day to that journey through the Bible. Oh what a joy it is to pick it up and read about people in the Old Testament, and then read about Jesus and the new covenant in the New Testament. You will find that you are just like the people in the Bible. You will find it is your story and we are all the same. You know why? We were all created in His image! (Genesis 1:26). You know why your stressful life is an abomination to you? It is an abomination to God! (Proverbs 11:1) Those are the types of truths we are going to discover in this section. When we have finished, we will not have studied all of God's Truths, but we will have studied enough of them to have learned how to go find more! God bless you as you enjoy every bit of this!

Day One – What does the creation story tell you about your creation?

Perhaps you grew up in church. Maybe you are familiar with all of the classic Bible stories. Maybe you have never been to church. Possibly, you are somewhere in between. I am going to approach this section in a way that takes nothing for granted. Remember, I asked you to clear your mind and look at all of this as fresh revelation from God. Whether this is a review or something new for you, soak it all in. You are going to be doing a lot of reading in this lesson. I hope you have a Bible you are comfortable with. You will be spending a lot of time with it!

1) Read Genesis 1. What does it say to you about Creation?

2) Read Genesis 2.

    a) How did God form man and how did man become a living being? (vs. 7)

    b) What did God do with man and what did God command and warn? (vs.15-17)

    c) What did God say was not good for man? (vs. 18)

    d) What did God provide for man? (vs. 18)

    e) How did God form woman? (vs. 21-22)

Men and women are different. While together they become and make one completed perfect union, they are different. Man does not have the capabilities of doing some of the things women do and vice versa. Why then do we waste so much time and energy beating each other up over our differences? Our differences should be celebrated, not sabotaged! There is a reason we sabotage each other's weaknesses. We are introduced to that reason in chapter 3!

    f) What is God's plan for the married couple? (vs. 24-25)

3) Read Genesis 3.

There is so much information in this chapter about the fall of man. There are so many questions about marriage that are answered right here in this chapter. Every time I read it, new things are revealed to me about another aspect of marriage. Rather than limit you to certain obvious situations, let me encourage you to spend the remainder of your time this morning allowing the Holy Spirit to reveal to you whatever He will about the fall of man and how the events in this chapter have influenced the course of marriage for mankind. Record your revelations. Trust me on this. As many times as you might revisit this chapter, (and I would encourage you to do that over and over again!), you will learn new and exciting things!

Day Two – Identity as a Christian

When I first wrote the husband and wife book, it was just the "wife" book. After years of teaching "the wife class" God started bringing couples to Ray and I to mentor. We had (and still have) no formal training in mentoring marriages. We were just willing and available. The only thing we had to share was our story of how God saved our marriage and how He continues to build it based on HIS Truths. As we prayed about how to help the couples that were being led to us, we started using the material in the wife book. It had a beginning and an end. It takes a couple through the same process God took us through. With just a few word changes, it was truly interchangeable and applicable to both. Ray had encouraged me for years that both men and women would benefit from this. The only way I could consider a husband and wife class was to be under Ray's authority and in his presence. I do not believe the entire testimony of scripture allows for women to teach with an attitude of spiritual authority over men. My research leads me to conclude women can prophesy and give instruction (or teach) in the church, as God surely gives the gift of prophecy and teaching to men and women. For me personally, I am only led to do such under my husbands authority and the authority of the spiritual leadership (Elders) of the church. This subject has been debated for thousands of years and not everyone interprets Paul's instructions to the church in Corinth and/or to Timothy with regards to what he was encountering at the church of Ephesus in the same way. For the purpose of this class, my only claim is as facilitator and witness to the things God has taught us about marriage, the Christian home, and family. That said, we will try as best we can to lead you to scripture that will help you seek your identity as a Christian man and Christian woman. Fair enough?

Have you ever heard someone say "he's a real man" or "she's a real woman?" What exactly is a real man or a real woman? Two thoughts come to mind when I ponder this question, culture and creation. Being a man or woman, according to culture can mean one thing, but being a man or woman according to creation can mean something totally different. Culture is man-made. Creation belongs to God. How disappointed and disillusioned would we be (not to mention confused!) if the truth (the Bible) changed with culture? The Bible, and its interpretation, is not meant to conform to culture. Culture should conform to the Bible. When we seek to define man or woman, we must look to scripture and creation, not culture and the world. We live in a world today where people have sex changes. We live in a world today where same sex marriages are flaunted and praised. The ones who shake their heads in disbelief are ridiculed as being in-tolerant people who just won't embrace diversity. So where does the Christian Man and Christian Woman get their identity?

Would it be a fair statement to say most of us have no idea where or how to seek our true identity? The truth is, most people (men & women) do not grow up learning exactly who we are created to be. Most of us end up resembling the people who raised us, and we become very much like the people we hang around. We are whatever our jobs/careers "tag" us to be and that is who we become. It is possible that God does not come into the picture at all. We are satisfied that going to church on Sundays makes us good enough, whatever that means. Meanwhile we struggle internally because we know, perhaps, that who we are is not who we think we should be. Yet we have no idea what that is, or how to become anything different than what we are. Even if we are "Christian" on Sundays, we do not know what that is supposed to mean Monday through Saturday.

The world is so full of choices. Today, more than ever, there are so many choices and opportunities for men and women. The sky is the limit. Literally! Women can go to the moon, men can be "Mr. moms" and the world teaches that our roles are interchangeable. Then why, please tell me, are men and women so miserable? May I? Because in our attempt to be just alike, being "just alike" is not what makes us happy, or holy. It is something our culture has made up and "it" has nothing to do with who we were created to be or what we were created to do. We are only ever happy, truly happy, and on our way to being holy, if we are fulfilling the purpose for which we were created. You do not have to agree with me. I am sharing with you what I have learned from searching the Bible, which I believe is the Holy Inerrant, Inspired, Infallible, Word of God.

The Bible teaches that Jesus Christ was born of a virgin. He was (and is) the son of God. He is (and was) fully man and fully God. He came that we might have life and have it more abundantly (John 10:10). He came to fulfill the law and the prophets. He died for our sins and was resurrected on the third day, which makes Him the living God. When man fell from God's grace, God, in His infinite wisdom, already had a plan for salvation. That plan restores man to God. It is done through His son, Jesus Christ. Jesus is "the way, the truth, and the life and no one comes to the Father except through Him." (John 14:6) Jesus is the door through which we find life. He says of Himself "If anyone enters by Me, he will be saved, and will go in and out and find pasture!" (John 10:9). Don't you love that? I don't know about you or what point you are in your life, but I reached a point in my marriage and home life where I was so miserable I couldn't get through that door quick enough to find that pasture! I wanted to be safe and secure. I didn't want to carry the burden any longer. I knew who the world was telling me to be. What the world was screaming seemed to be so contrary to what God was saying. I was so confused and very exhausted. Ray and I had no time for each other and really didn't even want to be around each other.

You know what Jesus says?

1) Read Matthew 11:28-29. Write those verses.

Can you run to Him fast enough? Do you want that rest? There are a lot of people on anti-depressant medications in our society today. I am not saying there is no need for it. If there is a physical/medical reason that causes someone to be depressed and medication is the answer, there is no shame in that. I wonder how many people, men, women, and children alike, are mis-diagnosed? I wonder how many people are, in fact, not depressed but exhausted? I wonder how many people need rest for their soul's? I shared with you in week two that just because I turned my marriage over to God, it didn't get better automatically. I shared things got worse for a while. I have also shared with you this is a process. I am now going to share with you there was a point in my life I was so exhausted and so tired of being whoever it was I was, I didn't want to live anymore. I would not have committed suicide because I personally believe I would have been saying to God that even He couldn't handle my problems. I did pray, however, for God to take me while my son was still young enough not to remember me! I didn't know who I was supposed to be. I was having an identity crisis. A lot of people have identity crisis.

God started showing me how to transform my mind, by reading His word. He started showing me that my nature should reflect His nature; my actions should bring glory to Him, not myself; and any accomplishments should further His purpose, not mine. He reminded me that I was a part of His world. I needed to stop trying to box Him into my world. My identity became clearer when I studied the teachings of Christ. Christianity has nothing to do with being male or female. It has everything to do with identifying with Christ, abiding in His word, studying and following His teachings, and becoming more Christ-like.

There was nothing about our marriage that represented a Christ-likeness. Our actions and words towards each other only confirmed the bitterness in our hearts. We wrongly believed our problems started with each other. We were starting in the wrong place. We needed to take our eyes off of each other and start with our individual relationship with God. Understanding who we are in HIM first as Christians, seeking our identity as Christian men and women, and understanding how things operate in His Kingdom, is the place to start.

2) Read Matthew 7:24-27. What does it say about the wise man? What does it say about the foolish man?

These verses come at the end of the Sermon on the Mount. The sayings He refers to are spread throughout the 5th, 6th, and 7th chapters of Matthew. There are, depending on how you count them, 33 or 34 sayings. Jesus is not merely sharing suggestions. He is giving commands. Webster's defines identity as the state or fact of being a specific person or thing. The "person" Jesus is commanding us to identify with is Himself. The "thing" he is commanding we become is a follower of His teachings. He tells us in Chapter 7: 24-27 that those who hear His sayings and do them are wise and even though the rain, flood, and winds come, their house won't fall because they have built themselves and their house on the solid foundation. But He warns that for those who hear His sayings and do not do them, the rains, floods, and winds will come and they and their house will fall. He warns that the fall is great. The rains, floods, and winds are the same for all of us. They are coming. Any one of us could be in the middle of one of those situations right now! What makes the difference is: are we identifying with Christ, are we following His teachings, and is He our foundation?

3) Spend the remainder of your time this morning reading Matthew, chapters 5, 6, and 7, and see how many of Jesus' sayings you can identify. Write them in your journal.

Day Three – Identity as a Christian husband and Christian wife

Yesterday we talked about how our identity as a Christian really has nothing to do with being male or female. Today, (and tomorrow), we are going to study our identity as Christian Husbands and Christian Wives. That has everything to do with being male and female. Get ready to scripture hunt! No commentary today. I am just going to give you the scriptures to read, and some room to write what you believe the Holy Spirit is telling you. This is not all inclusive by any means, but it will definitely paint you a picture of the different roles. Just read the scriptures and write what you think they say about the husband and wife. Before you start to read, I would encourage you to pray for the Holy Spirit - which is the Spirit of Truth - to reveal to your heart exactly what it is He wants you to know about the two roles. You are probably going to need to use your journals!

1) Genesis 2:15-25

2) Genesis 3:16-24

3) Deuteronomy 24:5 & Proverbs 31:10-31

4) Ephesians 5:25-33

5) Malachi 2:14-16

6) Matthew 5: 31-32

7) 1st Peter 3:7

8) Romans 12: 9-21. This pertains more to Christianity in general than to individual role assignments, none-the-less it is expected behavior

That is all for today. Aren't you learning some wonderful things? There is freedom in truth. My prayer is that you will start accepting this identity for yourself. It is important that you both get a mental picture of each other's role assignments. God clearly grants us equality in matters of inheritance, salvation, grace, love, justification, redemption, mercy, etc., but He also clearly calls each of us to gender specific roles/positions. We will learn as we continue in this study that God has a specific purpose and position for men and women. Please do not dwell on whether your spouse is fulfilling his or her role. Right now we are just gathering information. A time for application will come. Please start praying for yourself and your spouse to have an open heart to God's plan. You have no control over changing your spouse. You only have control over you. This is for you. Please do not be tempted to ponder how easy it would be to be what you are reading about if only your spouse would be what he or she is supposed to be. It doesn't work that way! You are going to have to go through a process regardless of what your spouse does or does not do. Have a great day and get a good night sleep. We have more of this tomorrow!

Day Four – Identity as a Christian husband and Christian wife

Are you ready to read and write some more today? Let's get right to it! You are probably going to need that journal again! How do these verses speak to Christian Identity?

1) 1st Corinthians 7:1-16

2) Ephesians Chapters 5 and 6

3) Colossians Chapter 3

4) Titus 2:1-8

5) Hebrews 11:1 and 6

6) Hebrews 12:1-2 (These two verses are encouraging and motivating to us as reminders of why we are doing what we are doing!)

7) 1st Peter 3:1-12 (I must stop and tell you that the scriptures you are about to read are the ones that changed our lives. It is still a favorite group of scriptures for me and whenever I feel the least bit negative, or sense that old nature rearing its ugly head, I can't get to this scripture fast enough!)

8) 1st Peter 5:1-11. In these verses Peter is talking to Christians in general and encouraging them to live according to Christ and not under the influence of neighbors and family members that are not Christian. As you read these verses, think about how you can specifically apply them in your marriage.

9) Finally the last one of the day! It is also from Peter. Can you tell I am a fan of Peter's? You know why I think I like Peter so much? I can relate to him. He was the disciple, you will remember, that denied Jesus three times before the cock crowed, just as Jesus predicted he would. Which one of us has not denied Jesus? The important part is, Peter didn't stop with the denial. He came back to Jesus and trusted Him as Lord and Savior. It was in reference to Peter, that Jesus said, "on this rock, I shall build my church."

For the final truth of the day, feast on 2nd Peter 1:1-11. It talks of fruitful growth in our faith. Just like the verses above, think about how you can specifically apply them in your marriage. This time, add what you believe the benefit of doing such would be. Record your thoughts in your journal.

Day Five - What happens when you try and your spouse does not?

This week we have studied the creation story, the identity of the Christian, and the identity of the Christian Husband and Wife. You should be inundated with truths about how you were created, who you should identify with as a Christian, and why that person is Jesus. You have read a ton of scripture about your identity as a Christian husband and wife. You might be questioning what if I make all of these changes, really try my best, and my spouse doesn't even try to seek the truth, much less try to change? You want the truth? That might very well happen. Let me explain.

You have been taking this class now for 5 weeks. If your spouse has seen any changes in your behavior towards him or her, they might be wondering how long it will last. If your marriage is anything at all like ours was, it is going to take longer than 5 weeks to convince your spouse you have changed. Remember, this is not about your spouse. It is about you. It is about you serving your Lord Jesus Christ. It is about your Christianity. It is about your commitment to God. You have no control over what your spouse does or does not become. Here's the good part. Neither will you be held accountable for what he/she does or does not become. We will all stand before His throne one day. We will all be held accountable as individuals. God is not going to buy any excuses! When He asks me to give an account of my life, I am not going to be able to say "well God I would have become what you wanted me to be if Ray had have lived up to your expectations for him." Five weeks of this study, regardless of what type of changes it may have produced thus far, is just not enough for your spouse to take seriously at this point. If you should stick with this new way of life for 6 months, all it will take to shake their trust is one little "old nature" back sliding bark, and you will have taken two steps forward and three steps backward.

I am not suggesting it is all up to you. When I started this journey I didn't think about what Ray thought. He didn't know about the changes taking place in my heart. I was still plenty "bruised" from the mess we had made of our marriage. My quest was strictly to heal me and discover the truth. If Ray was blessed in the process, good for him! I needed to be healed, strengthened, and established in the truths of God. I could no longer live that old life. I was not going to live miserable in the same house with my husband for the rest of my life. I knew Ray didn't want that either. Most of all, I knew that was not what God had in mind for marriage. We have to get to a point in our walk with God that it doesn't matter what the other person does or does not do. We have to entrust our spouse to God and trust God to have His way with us.

Here is what I want you to think about. If you are seeking the truth and sense that your spouse is not, does that change the truth? Does what you do have anything to do with what he or she does not do? Did God create both of you? Does God love you both the same? Do you have the right to disrespect and/or disregard one of God's created beings? Do you have any rights, or do you have responsibilities to God? These are just some questions to get you thinking about how it does not change your responsibilities to God just because you might try and your spouse does not. Admittedly, if only one is trying, it will make for a bigger challenge! However, God is a very big God and there is nothing too great for him. Did my husband change? Yes. Did I change? Yes. Do we still have challenges? Yes. But let me assure you our lives are not even close to being what they used to be. We are so amazed at the changes that have taken place.

God doesn't want us to stay married just for the sake of being married and being miserable. He wants to bless us and show others how He intends marriage to be. He doesn't want to bless us just for our sake. He wants us to be His witnesses in a hurting world testifying to His glory! He is our hope! There is no other relationship like the marital relationship! God compares it to Christ and the Church! It is intended to be a place of blessing! It is intended to be a place of peace and a showcase of spiritual fruit! It is supposed to be the place for God to raise Godly offspring. A marriage that exemplifies God's intent is comparable to nothing any greater than we can know this side of glory. If that product has to start in my heart in my home, it should not matter if or when my spouse gets on board! God calls me to obedience regardless of what anyone else does. We should all be praying for every member of our households to get on board with obedience to God. Whether they do or not, we have no control, but we can find peace in knowing God will bless our own obedience.

Today is going to be an easy day. You have worked very hard this week. Use the remainder of your time this morning to finish any previous work you may not have finished. If you are caught up, just ponder how wonderful your marriage could be based on what you have learned thus far. Spend time with God. Ask God to let you know if you are on the right path. Next week we are going to study God's definition of love and marriage. Start praying for God to open your heart and mind to His ideal for love and marriage. Ask Him to make it well with your soul.

WEEK
Six

Love, Marriage, Family

Last week was not for the "faint at heart" as I like to say. When I was introduced to those scriptures years ago, I became right indignant! The more I read about the wife being submissive to the husband, the more indignant I became. The more I read about being tender hearted, kind, showing brotherly love, and being courteous to my husband, the uglier I got! While I am very convicted and ashamed to admit it now, I loved having pity party's complaining to God about what I thought Ray should be doing. Well ... a funny thing happened on the way to a pity party one day. As I was starting off my quiet time complaining to God, and once I had finished ranting and raving in my prayer time and journal entry, God led me to 1st Peter 3:12. Let's read it together: "For the eyes of the Lord are on the righteous, and His ears are open to their prayers; But the face of the Lord is against those who do evil." OH MY GOSH! A terror gripped my heart.

All of the sudden, I realized God was not even listening to my complaints about Ray. The scripture says "the eyes of the Lord are on the righteous and His ears are open to their prayers." I was anything but righteous. The only classification of righteous I fell into was "self" as in self-righteous, which as we know, is entirely evil. I found myself facing the truth that says "the face of the Lord was against those (me) who do evil." This revelation put a different slant on the situation. See, it was easy for me to be ugly to Ray when I thought Ray was the one getting what he deserved. This little twist threw a totally new level of accountability on me! When it was Ray that I directed my anger towards, I didn't fear the consequences. When I started understanding the problem I was having was really with God, I started to get scared! God had my attention. He made it crystal clear to me that it didn't matter what I thought Ray was deserving of, God commanded me to treat him with a specific type of respect. He started revealing that my conduct, as a Christian, was not an option, nor was it based on whether someone deserved it or not. That, my friend, is something to fear!

As I searched and searched the scriptures (most of the ones we studied last week), I gained a totally new perspective on who I was and what was expected of me as a Christian and a Christian wife! I stopped participating in the "husband/wife jokes" and made it clear to others around me that I couldn't participate anymore. I stopped complaining publicly AND PRIVATELY, about the things that irritated me about Ray. I went to God every morning with a spirit of thanksgiving and still do! I keep the negative to myself. If I absolutely have to talk about something, I make sure I talk to God about Ray with as much respect as I can. I DO NOT HAVE THE RIGHT TO DEMEAN OR DEGRADE ANOTHER CREATED BEING OF GOD - ESPECIALLY ANOTHER CHRISTIAN! That includes my husband. That especially includes my husband. Did this revelation make me love Ray anymore? Did all of the irritations go away because of this revelation? No. However, it did allow me to respect him. I had to ask God to forgive me for the way I thought about and disrespected Ray. I eventually mustered up enough courage to share this with Ray and ask for his forgiveness.

Why do I tell you this? Because I know I am not alone. I know there are many who could tell the same story. I know there are many of you reading this right now, perhaps even crying, because this describes your relationship. I know how painful it is. You might be thinking, "I don't love him/her, can't love him/her, won't ever love him/her anymore, but neither can I imagine God wants us to divorce." You feel like you are between a rock and a hard place. You're right.

You are between a rock and a hard place. The rock was my hardened heart. The hard place was coming to the realization I had been sinning against God by turning my back on His Word. What I did next was what saved our marriage and brought peace to my heart and our relationship. I asked forgiveness, repented of my sin, and walked a different walk. It doesn't mean I have not erred. I have. But I no longer live that lifestyle as a matter of practice. Our lives changed. Our relationship changed. I have never asked my husband to change. The change had to happen in my heart first. The manifestation of that has been, and continues to be, worked out daily, in the things I say and do. Do I mess up? Yes. The difference is, I recognize those mess ups instantly and make all effort to correct them immediately.

The things we studied last week should have given you a clearer picture of what a Christian marriage is intended to be. The conduct that was described in so many of those scriptures, if adhered to, would create an environment where love thrives. Can you imagine living in a home where the utmost respect is shown to all, by all? Can you imagine a home where the husband is to the wife what Christ is to the church? Can you imagine a home where the husband is so understanding of the wife that his prayers are not hindered because he treats her the way God has commanded him to treat her? Can you imagine a home where husband reveres God, wife respects husband, and children respect, honor, and obey the parents? That is what I am talking about. That is what God is talking about. That is what He intended our marriages and our homes to be!

What we studied last week was truth! My guess is, you like me, didn't learn that in school. We didn't learn it watching T.V., and we didn't, sad to say, learn it in church. I only learned it as I searched the scriptures, and perhaps you are just learning it for the first time. My search gave me a hunger to know more. I wanted that type of marriage. I wanted to live like that. I wanted a husband like I read about in the Bible, and I knew he wanted a wife like he read about in the Bible. Before I got married I thought all it took to have a successful marriage was "love." You probably did too. My definition of love, I have come to learn, was an emotional type of love. If I felt "good" about him, it meant I loved him. If I didn't feel "good" about or towards him, it meant I didn't love him. Based on that definition of love, I did "not" love him a whole lot more than I did love him! If I loved him, my treatment towards him was good. If I did not love him, my treatment towards him was terrible! Can you guess what it was most of the time? It was terrible. I knew what I thought love was. It was this chemistry between a man and a woman that lasted a lifetime if it was a true love. It had everything to do with the way they treated each other. It was something that was automatic and romantic and it came from within. That's what the world would have us believe. God has a different definition of love and there is nothing automatic or romantic about it. It can become automatic and yes, it can even become romantic, but "it" is an intentional act, and yes, it is a decision!

This week we are going to explore God's truths about love, marriage, and family. When we know the truth, we can live according to truth. We can meditate inside of God's will for our lives. We can focus on God's way and leave behind the unrealistic false images we have been worshipping all our lives. Here is the best part. We can live without regrets! Did you hear that? When we live inside of God's will, we live regret free lives. Praise God, what a blessing that is. Get your reading and writing supplies ready! We're going to have another glorious week in the Word of God.

Day One – What is love?

We have already talked about what you think love is and what made you think you were in love with your spouse. Today, we are going to look at that a little more closely because we want to compare your definition with God's.

1) How do you define love?

2) How do you think your spouse defines love?

3) What made you think you and your spouse were in love before you got married?

4) Have you fallen out of love with each other? If so, when and how do you think that happened?

5) How does God define Love? What do you base your answer on?

6) Read 1st Corinthians 13. What does that chapter say about love?

7) Is your definition of love in line with the Word of God in 1st Corinthians 13? How are they alike and/or different?

8) What do you have to change about yourself to "love" your spouse according to God's definition?

Day Two – What is this thing called marriage all about?

Did you have any idea what marriage was really all about before you got married? I was at a wedding about twenty (plus) years ago and I was so impressed by something the preacher said. He told the bride and groom that in ten years, he would be able to look at them and know she will have become what he (the groom) had helped her to become, and he (the groom) will have become what she (the bride) will have helped him to become. There is so much truth in that. I have become what my husband has influenced me to become, good and bad, and he has become what I have influenced him to become. What we have helped (or hurt) each other to be, has not been the only influence, but it has been a big influence. Marriage is a difficult journey. If we are not sure what it is meant to be, we make mistake after mistake. We damage each other and the children. The damage goes beyond the family. It affects society and the very culture we live in. When families are strong and healthy, the nation is strong and healthy. When we cherish each other, we cherish our values. Who we are and our way of life is worth preserving. When we are fighting among ourselves, we are seeking selfish gain, values are gone and our way of life is no longer worth preserving. When that happens, cultures / societies crumble. All we have to do is look around us. America has changed so much in just the last 10 years, I believe, because while we say we are a Christian nation, it doesn't look like Christianity at all.

Today we are going to take a look at God's definition of marriage. We will be revisiting some of the verses of scripture you looked at last week. We need to get a clear mental picture of what marriage was intended to look like, according to God. When we know what something looks like, we can move towards making our homes and marriages look like it. Will your marriage ever be what it is supposed to be? Only you can answer that question. All of our marriages can be what they are supposed to be. It is up to us to run towards the goal. You cannot use the excuse that yours will never be what it is supposed to be because your spouse is not willing to change. The change will never take place if you do not change. So what if you have to go first?

Remember, pride comes before the fall. Wouldn't you hate for your family to trip over your pride? I know I would. It just doesn't matter what he or she does. You are called to be what you are called to be and you are accountable to God for that. As long as I am married, which is until death do we part, I am called to live according to God's commands. He has commands for marriage. Let's take a look at exactly what that is.

1) Read Genesis 2: 24-25. What does that mean?

2) How does a man leave his mother and father and cling to his wife?

3) Describe your relationship with your in-laws.

4) Describe your spouse's relationship with their parents. What was that family life like?

5) Describe your relationship with your parents. What was your family life like?

6) Describe your spouse's relationship with your parents.

7) Do any of the relationships you have described above, conflict with God's intent for the husband and wife to leave the relationship of parents behind and cling to one another as "one?" Explain your answer.

Spend the remainder of your time this morning in prayer with God asking Him to reveal to you anything that might need to change with regards to parental influence that could be hindering you from becoming "one" with each other. Record your thoughts and prayers.

Day Three – This thing called marriage ... continued

There are a lot of couples that have found it very difficult to leave their parents "mentally" and focus on becoming a family of their own with their spouse. If you grew up in a home where there was a parent with a very domineering personality, it is very difficult to stop trying to live your life to please that person. It doesn't matter that you are married and living under another roof. That parental influence might be so strong it is not only still controlling you, it is trying to control your spouse. If you have children, it is even infiltrating the troops! God says "stop it." You are "one" with your spouse and you are to leave your parents. Does that mean you don't have a relationship with them any longer? Does that mean you have to stop loving them? NO! But it does mean you and your spouse run your home, not your parents (and, might I add, neither are the children supposed to run the home!). So how do you do that? Just keep on reading and studying the Truth! Focus your mind on God and continue to learn what a marriage and Christian home looks like according to His Word. You don't have to announce to your parents or in-laws that you are going to start doing things differently. Just start living according to the way God is leading you, and you will be amazed at how things will change. Remember, God blesses obedience. There might come a time where you have to have a "talk" with them, but God will let you know if and when that is necessary.

Read Ephesians 5: 15-33. Answer the following questions:

1) vs. 15-16. How are we supposed to walk? Why do we have to be mindful of the times?

2) vs. 17-20. Whose "will" should we be concerned with? What should we be filled with? How are we supposed to speak to one another? Who are we to give thanks to for what and when?

3) vs. 21. Who are we supposed to submit to and why?

4) vs. 22 - 24. What is the wife instructed to do? Why? What is the husband/ wife relationship compared to?

5) vs. 25-31. What is the husband instructed to do? Why? Describe the way a husband should love his wife.

6) vs. 32-33. Describe the way you think Christ loves the church. With that in mind, why do you think the husband is exhorted to love his wife and the wife is exhorted to respect her husband?

Spend the remainder of your time in prayer with God, asking Him to show you ways that your marriage already resembles the passages of scripture we've read today. If there are not many, or any resemblances, ask God to start showing you how you might need to change to incorporate this picture of marriage in your heart. Write in your journal what you feel He is teaching you.

Day Four – Instructions for husbands and wives – the beginning of the family blessings

Are you beginning to see how God's plan for the family follows a particular order? Does it mean any one family member is more important than the other? No. It means God is a very orderly God and He has a special system for the family. When that system and order is followed, the family is so blessed. When that order is not followed, there is utter chaos. God calls families to a blessing. The family starts with God, then husband and wife. When husband and wife understand and obey the instructions of God, they are blessed. Those blessings are poured through them to the children. Let's take a look at those instructions and blessings.

Read 1st Peter 3:1-12. These verses give instruction to the husband and the wife and in the end it promises blessings to those that turn away from evil and seek to do good. Peter is talking to Christian couples here. He is not talking to pagan worshippers. He is talking to you and me. He is clear about who God listens to and who God turns His face away from. We have already looked at these verses in an earlier lesson, but it is worth going back to. Concentrate on the following verses and write what you think the instructions are.

1) vs. 1-4 - what is Peter saying to the wife? What is precious to God?

2) vs. 7 - what is Peter saying to the husband? What happens to the husband's prayers if he obeys this?

3) Concentrate on vs. 8-12 for the remainder of your time this morning. Write down all of the instructive commands and all of the promises if adhered to. What would your home life be like if everyone in your house abided by these instructions? Record your thoughts in your journal

Day Five – The family order – the Christian home

I know we can all agree on this one thing ... where there is God-less-ness, there is man-made-mess. I can tell a distinct difference between a home where God is the center, and one where He is not. To be even more precise, I can tell a difference between a home where God is the center and one where He is not, even if the one where He is not, the family goes to church. Did you get what I just said? Is it possible to be a church going family and still live in a man-made-mess? It is not only possible, friend, it is probable if all that is "Christian" about the family is that they go to church. Going to church does not make a family a Christian family. It just means the family goes to church. Granted, it is a great start! But, going to church does not mean biblical growth is being sought or applied to the family's Monday through Saturday routine. A strong, united, loving family doesn't just happen. It, too, is intentional and it takes work and study! Relationship, relationship, relationship! It is all about relationship. The first and most important relationship is the one you and each family member have with God. If you are not seeking a personal relationship with God through Jesus Christ, which is what the Christian faith teaches, (no one cometh unto the Father except through the son, John 14:6), then you might be going to church, but you are not seeking or applying biblical growth to your life or your family. Your growth has to start with you! So much of Christian instruction is focused on conduct. We are going to look at the third chapter of Colossians and learn what we are supposed to do, and what we are not supposed to do, to make our homes Christian homes.

Read Colossians 3:1-4.

1) What are we reminded of and what are we instructed to set our mind upon? Why?

2) vs. 5-11. What are the behaviors we are to put to death and get rid of? How is the "new man" described (vs. 10-11)?

3) vs. 12-13. As believers and followers of Christ, what should our conduct look like inside our homes?

4) vs. 14 - Above all, what is the most important and why?

5) vs. 15 - What should rule in our hearts and what should our attitudes be?

6) vs. 16-17 - What are we instructed to do?

7) vs. 18-21 - What does the family order look like and what is each member instructed to do?

8) vs. 23-25 - How are we supposed to do that which we are called to do? Who do we receive our reward from? Who do we serve? What happens to those who do wrong?

This week we have looked at love, marriage, and the family according to God's truths in scripture. Spend the remainder of your time this morning going back over your answers. Draw your own prayerful conclusions about the benefits of allowing God to build your love, marriage, and family on His principles and in His Righteousness. God delivers us in His Righteousness and does all of His work in Truth. You are His work. Your marriage is HIS work. Allow Him to build you. Record your thoughts in your journal.

WEEK
Seven
A Time to Reflect

This, as you know, is a twelve week course. The first week should have been used as a time of introduction to the course and to each other. Weeks two through six are what you have just finished. Those lessons were designed to take you through a process. It is a good chance you have had a lot of questions answered. Perhaps you have been challenged to think about life in a way you have never thought of before. This is all very real. A time of decision is coming. I thought it was important to allow a week of reflection. Please take the time this week to go back over each lesson. Pray about the things you have discovered about yourself, your spouse, your life, your marriage, and Christianity. I have provided a very short guide to help you with this process. You will be using your journals to record your answers. Next week, and for the remainder of this course, we will look at making some concrete decisions and applications for positive changes in our lives. What you reflect on this week, will help you with those decisions! Discuss your answers with your spouse. Pray together.

Day One – Reflections from Week Two

Review Week Two. What was the most important thing you learned about yourself, about life, about others? Are you ready to turn your marriage over to God?

Day Two - Reflections from Week Three

Review Week Three. What did you learn about the false images in your life? Are you prepared to move forward with the understanding you no longer have to be controlled by the false images of your past? Explain your answer.

Day Three - Reflections from Week Four

Review Week Four. This lesson takes a good look at the truth of life as you have come to know it. The honeymoon is really over. You both know what the other one is really like.

Take the time to honestly answer what type of marriage you have. Most marriages are irritable, therefore they can be salvaged! What would your marriage be like if both of you were seeking God and earnestly becoming what He intended you to become? Would your marriage move from the irritable category to the irreplaceable? Do you want that to happen? Explain your answer.

Day Four – Reflections from Week Five

Review Week Five. This lesson introduced us to the truth about our creation, marriage, and identity - according to God. What was the most important thing you learned? Was there anything that you found difficult to accept? Explain your answer. Was any of this new information to you? Explain your answer.

Day Five – Reflections from Week Six

Review Week Six. This lesson talked about the biblical view of love, marriage, husbands and wives, and the Christian home. How do your ideas of those things compare to what you learned from the Bible? Which way is a better way for your family to live? Explain your answer. What, if anything, has to change in your life for your family to enjoy the life God intended?

Hopefully, you have learned a lot this week. Next week, and for the remainder of this course, we will only benefit from what we will learn if we commit to accepting God's way of life. To this point we have learned how we live, why we live like we do, and what God's truths say about how we should live. No change has been required. We have merely been collecting information. For positive change to take place, we have to act on what we have learned. If you are not going to divorce, or merely exist in the same house with each other, and if you are truly serious about turning your marriage over to God, accepting and applying the principles in the last four sessions is a great place to start!

WEEK
Eight

Decision Time: Accepting God's Vision for yourself, your marriage, and family

Wasn't it enough just to read the truth? Did I have to challenge you to accept it? Yes. I had to challenge you to accept it. We are all challenged to accept the truth. At some point we have to decide to live according to God's truths or stay stuck in our sins. When we see the truth of what we have become, beside the truth of what God created us to become, we must know there is another step. It doesn't stop with just knowing the Truth. You and I have to decide we are either going to ignore God's truths and continue living with our false images, or we are going to accept His vision for our lives and live accordingly.

God gives us a free will to choose how we will live. We have just finished two studies. In weeks three and four we looked at the bare bones truth about who we are and how we got there. In weeks five and six, we looked at God's truths about who He created us to be and how we are supposed to live, love, and be Christian families. In week two, we learned we are all pretty much alike and face the same challenges. We all face the same decision. Either we are going to accept God's vision for our lives, or we are not. If we accept His vision, does that mean we can automatically go about living it and it will be easy to do? Ha! If your decision is to go on living life as usual, does that mean life will be any easier? Ha! Either way presents its own challenges. I must be truthful and tell you by accepting God's vision, we are assured His help. I can't tell you what will happen if you decide not to choose His way. That wasn't my decision. I am so thankful. I can imagine my marriage would have ended in divorce. Had we have stayed together and not pursued God's plan, I can't begin to imagine the turmoil my family would have suffered. I am so grateful unto God that He has shown us another way.

You might be asking yourself, why is it so important to follow God's vision? Maybe you complain about your marriage and home life a little. Maybe you complain a lot, but it works okay for the most part. Besides, you can go on living like you are and serving God at your church. You don't need your spouse for that. You don't need your children for that. It is the life you live outside of your family. They probably have their own "thing" too, right? Can I go out on a limb here? Can I say that just because that's what 99% of the other church people do, (that's my opinion), it doesn't make it right. We are so comfortable in our ruts and sin. There are times when we get so defeated by the struggle we just want to forget it is something we need to work on. We don't want to put forth the effort. It becomes a very tolerable way of life. The real sad part is our Christian world is so full of that, that the world can't tell the difference between Christian families and non-Christian families. Shame, Shame, Shame on us.

We have to set ourselves, our marriages, our families, and our homes apart from the rest of the world. We have to be the salt of the earth. (Matthew 5:13) We have to be the light of the world (Matthew 5: 14). Jesus tells us we are those things. Our marriages and families must glorify God. All that we are must bring glory to God. It does matter that we argue, fuss, and fight with our spouses and children, and then put on our happy ministerial faces and go to church. God knows we are phonies! Our spouses and children know we are phonies. We know we are phonies! You get involved in your church, give it some time, and everyone at church will know you are a phony! So you see? There is no place to hide. There is no decision really, other than to accept God's vision for your life and allow HIM to work in you. He will reveal HIMSELF to you. In this lesson, we are going to concentrate on how to accept, discover, and live God's vision for yourself, your marriage, and your family.

Day One – Surrender of Self

I am going to share the secret of success with you right here. We have made it past half of the workbook now, so we deserve to know the secret. The secret of the success of living a life that brings glory to God is SURRENDER! You surrender yourself to Him. It has to start there. I have to lay down my life, my selfish desires, my demands, my wants, my dreams, my attitudes, my sin, my, my, my everything and empty myself of me. It has to start with God and me, not me and Ray, not church, not family. It starts with God and me. That is not hard to do when we are sick of ourselves and everything about our life. It is very hard to do when we are self- centered and like it! That's called living in our sin and being comfortable in it! We all know which side of the coin we are on. He wants us surrendered and self-less.

So how do you do that? How many times have you given up something like a habit or an attitude, or promised to go on a diet, and taken it all back as soon as the temptation became too great? I just love those people who say "I just gave it to the Lord and that was that!" "Just give it to the Lord and He will take care of it!" they say. What does that mean? We can't exactly put our spouse in a box and ship them off to heaven can we? I can see the note attached now -

Dear God,

Here is my spouse- please do something with him/her - I give up! And when you send them back, could you make sure he/she does exactly what you say to do? Or, better yet, could you make sure he/she does exactly what I say to do? Thanks!

Sincerely,
Yours Truly

Is that how you give something to God? There may be many ways to do it. I only know of one. I can only share with you how I have learned to do this in my marriage. I have to constantly work on it, I might add! It is ongoing and I will confess I do not always succeed. I have not experienced victory in every area of my life. Only the areas that I have been able to totally surrender to God have I found victory. Here is how I have learned to do it.

I have a quiet time every day. In that quiet time, I meet God. I meet with God. I pray to God. I journal to God. I listen to God by sitting still in His presence and just concentrating on knowing that He is God. I listen to God by reading His word, studying His word, and learning His word. I write down the things I believe He is teaching me through His word. I write down what I believe the scripture means as it applies to me and my life. I ponder His word. I meditate in and on His word. I worship God. I praise God. I thank God for everything - good and bad. That is how I have a quiet time and that is where my surrender begins daily. It is a daily event and a daily surrender. Would you believe ... I still fall? Would you believe with all of that "spirituality" I still have times of defeat and sin? Even so, there is still nothing sweeter than abiding in HIS Word, all alone, just the two of us.

I find such encouragement and instruction in the words of Peter, divinely inspired by God, as he writes in 1st Peter 5:1-11. Let's read those verses.

1) Peter encourages us to submit to one another and be clothed in humility. Why? vs. 5

God resists the _____, but gives _____ to the _____.

Peter tells the younger people to submit to the elders, and all of us to submit to one another. Does that mean, could that possibly mean husbands and wives too? Could that possibly mean that as parents we are to stop thinking of our children as "subjects" and start respecting them as people? Let's think about this. You mean it is not okay for me to speak to my spouse or children in a disrespectful manner? You mean I need to treat them with as much respect as I would my pastor, pastor's wife, and their children? That's exactly what it means. God resists the proud and gives grace to the humble. Let's go on ...

2) vs. 6 & 7

Therefore _____ yourselves under the mighty hand of God, that He may

_____ you in due time, casting all your _____ upon Him, for He

_____ for you.

It is not important to "win" the argument and belittle the people you live with. If that is what you are doing, if you are trying to be exalted in their eyes, you're losing! When we humble ourselves under His hand (surrender ourselves - our need to be our own god) He will exalt us and bring Glory to Himself, when the time is right for Him. We just need to cast all our care on Him, for He cares for us. To humble ourselves and cast all our care on Him is a surrendering of self to God!

3) vs. 8

Be _____, be _____, because your adversary the _____

walks about like a roaring lion seeking whom he may _____.

The reason we need to meet with God daily and surrender ourselves unto Him, the reason we must be sober and on guard, diligent and persistent, is because there is an adversary the devil that walks about like a roaring lion seeking whom he may devour. He is not particular. He will devour anyone he can. He will devour you. He will devour your home. He will devour your children. He will devour anything that could otherwise bring glory to God. Can one hour at church on Sunday morning prepare you to fight against the wiles of the devil? No. Yet that is all of the spiritual food most Christians get each week, if that! Then we wonder why our Christianity doesn't make a difference in our lives? Why would it? Would one meal keep us fed physically for a week? NO! Neither will one sermon keep us surrendered, sober, on guard, diligent, and persistent. It has to be a sober, diligent, persistent, purposeful act every day to meet with God and to surrender ourselves so that He can do what He promises as we read on.

4) vs. 9-10

Resist him (the devil), steadfast in the faith knowing that the same _____ are experienced by your brotherhood in the _____. But may the God of all _____, who called us to His _____ glory by _____ _____, after you have suffered a while, _____, _____, _____, and _____ you.

We need that power, that daily power to resist the devil, stand fast in our faith, knowing that the same sufferings are experienced by our brothers (and sisters!) in the world! We are all alike ... and guess what? This same information applies to our spouse and children!

Did you hear that? They have the same struggles. Why do we think they don't? Or that they should be treated with any less respect and empathy than anyone else who struggles? Or that they are capable of being perfect any more than we are? God, who is the God of all grace, who called us to His eternal glory by Christ Jesus - calls our husbands and children too, with that same grace, to that same eternal glory by the same Christ Jesus! After we (and they!) have suffered (and surrendered) a while, God will perfect, establish, strengthen, and settle us! To Him be the glory and the dominion forever and ever. Amen!

Don't you love that "settle you" part at the end of verse 10? That is what being surrendered means, being settled. "I'm settled Lord, I'm yours." I am surrendered. Here I am. Perfect me, establish the me you want me to be, strengthen me Lord settle me! Does that not comfort your soul? Does that not bring a peace over you? When you are surrendered, the one you have surrendered to has complete charge over you. He is completely responsible for the outcome. It is in His hands. You are in His hands. All your care has been cast on Him because He cares for you. The question then, comes down to, do we trust Him enough to thrust our care upon Him? Ah! Now we're getting somewhere! We will look at the issue of Trust tomorrow. For the remainder of the day, let me suggest you feast on James 4:7-10. Peter wasn't the only one who knew (or taught) that humility (or surrender) could cure worldliness. James taught the same thing. Read what he has to say about it. James was the half-brother of Jesus! He lived with him! We can live with Him too, as He lives in us, we must abide in Him, daily.

Day Two - Trust

Oh boy! This is a good one! There are several definitions of the word trust. My Webster's New World Dictionary defines trust as a firm belief in the honesty, reliability, etc. of another; faith; the confident expectation, hope, etc.; care; custody; to commit something to a person's care. Now, we could concentrate on any one of those, but for this study, today, I want to concentrate on care, custody, and committing something to a person's care. Yesterday we looked at 1st Peter 5:7 which say's "casting all your care upon Him for He cares for you." Today, we are going to explore casting or committing all our care on God.

Notice the New King James Version says "all your care" - not cares. NIV says "Cast all your anxiety on him because he cares for you." NASB says "Casting all your anxiety on him because he cares for you." Why do I share these different translations? While I prefer the New King James translation, I know I might not be in the majority. I wanted to be sure to capture all of the popular translations here to paint the picture of exactly what it is God is commanding as we talk about trusting Him. If we are going to commit all of our care and anxiety to God, if we are going to commit our custody into His hands, I want to make sure we know what we are doing.

What would your reaction be if I said to you "entrust your care (your very being) to me, and I will take care of you!" My guess is some would say "sold!" Some of you would say "what are you going to do?" Some would even say "that's okay I'll take care of myself." Mostly, there would be skepticism. Let me share something with you guys about women. This can give you some insight you might find helpful. If I have learned one thing about women over the last twenty+ years, it is this, a woman will do most anything to be secure. Secure in what? Her house, her life, her motherhood, her job, her church, her finances, her marriage, other relationships, HER VERY BEING! How will a woman find security in those things? By being in CONTROL! Uh oh! Ouch! I just stepped on some toes. The truth is, women like being in control. The way we do things might not be the best way to do them, but if we are in control, we usually have a safe and sure outcome.

Let me give you an example. Let's take finances for instance. If I control the checkbook, I know everything is not only going to get paid, it is going to get paid on time. I know how much money we have, what we need to live on, and what we can spend on entertainment. I can play it safe, or do something special this weekend. I can spend a little more money than normal, because I know the deposit is going in the bank on Monday. As long as I am in control, I am fine. It doesn't matter to me that my husband has to ask me for money - or that I scrutinize everything he wants to spend money on. It doesn't matter, that I tell him we can't afford the $50 extra dollars he wants to spend this week, yet I justify the $50 I decide to spend a day later on something I "need." In fact, I treat him and his money requests just like I do the children when they ask for something. I can justify it all. I am in control. I trust no one but myself with the finances. It might not be the best way to handle them. I might not be the best financial planner in the world where my family's future is concerned, but it is safe! I can live with safe!

If that describes your household, while you are living with "safe" everybody else in your house is living in submission to you. It might work for you and your household. It might even be okay with your husband because "he's not interested in handling the finances," but let me tell you, it is not God's plan. God would have everyone in the family be submissive to Him. God would have everyone in the family know that He is in control. If the person in "control" is not living in submission to God, it is a good chance, no one in the house is. I used the finances as an example. It could be other things that say "I'm in control" in your house. As in any area of life, if we are not following God's plan for it, we are not experiencing the blessings of God. The family misses those blessings too. Then, we are just like the world. I speak from experience. There are areas I am not experiencing His blessings in. You know why? I TRUST ME WITH THAT AREA MORE THAN I TRUST GOD!

I can say that because I am telling you the truth about me. I like control. As I have done a lot of the "image" studies through the years, I have learned one thing about me if I have learned nothing else. The root of all of my emotional, physical, spiritual, and relational problems stems from my desire, need, obsession, and compulsion to be in control. Here is the kicker! I consider myself to be in the "norm" of women in society. If that is the root of my evil, and if I am in the norm, my guess is there are plenty of other women in the same boat! I share that with you men because it is helpful to know that about women. If your wife demonstrates the same characteristics, please know that she does what she does because she wants to be secure. If she finds that security in your leadership, you will likely see the control issues disappear.

Keep in mind, most of the people I meet are in the church. We are in a Christian environment. The stories are the same. This is her mindset: She has to run the household, because she thinks her husband is not the leader God would have him be. WE have to be in control. WE don't trust our husbands to be in control. There is no telling what our households would be like if control were given (by us!) to our husbands. Guess what? The headship of the family is not the wife's to give! It is God's to give and He already gave that to the man. I was out of compliance with God and Ray! It is not anymore mine to give, than it is Ray's to reject! WE are both accountable to God for how we obey or disobey the "order" and the "individual responsibilities" He has given us to follow in our marriage and home! WOE! That meant I had to start trusting God! That meant I had to start trusting God's plan! That meant I had to cast all my care, worries, anxiety (especially for my household - which was my life!) on God and I couldn't be in charge of them anymore! That was too big of a request. It was a lot easier to stay mad with Ray because he wouldn't "lead" (the way I wanted him to) than it was to trust God with all of my anxieties. Here is the truth. We are comfortable in that sin because it is a lot easier to blame someone else, making ourselves look like the hero, than it is to repent of the sin and trust God.

Did I have to go there? If I am the only one who is guilty of the situation I just described, I am so sorry. If you do not find yourself in that scenario, please go onto the next section. I read sections of scripture that back up what I just said (Genesis 2:18 / Genesis 3:16-17, Ephesians 5:21-31). I am not going to elaborate on them just now because we studied them in Week Five. Please go back and read them if you are having trouble digesting what I have shared. I had trouble digesting it too. But it was all much more productive for me when I realized it was God I had the challenge with and not Ray. How could that be you ask? How could it be more productive to know your challenge is with God and not someone else? If you go to the source, you'll find the solution. It didn't have as much to do with how much I did or did not trust Ray, as it did with how little I trusted God.

The second step in accepting God's vision for my life is accepting the fact that I need to learn how to TRUST GOD! This, just like surrendering of self, is a daily, if not minute by minute, decision and matter of obedience. Have you ever wondered if God has the same question of us that we have of HIM? Is it not true that what we really ask is "God, can I really trust you?" And, isn't that what He wants to know and be assured of with us? "Robin, can I trust you to obey me?" If I am waking up every morning and asking God "can I trust you?" and He is asking me the same, where and how do we begin building that "trust" relationship? Quiet time, Quiet time, Quiet time! Here again, I can only share with you the way I attempt to build that trust and relationship. I have to go to the Word of God to see what He says about trusting Him. Then I have to journal about my life and remind myself how God has always taken care of me. Then I have to pray and thank Him and praise Him for all that He is to me. It is through that praise and thanksgiving that I begin to sense His peace and comfort as He begins settling my heart and mind. It is in that atmosphere that a trust-relationship is born.

As important as it is to be in a Bible study group, like a Sunday school class, and as important as it is to be in worship service in church on Sundays, I do not get that personal relationship building opportunity in those group settings. You might. Jesus was in many group settings according to the gospels. But when it counted the most, when He needed something special, He went to His Father alone. I have to do the same thing. There are many good resources available to teach us how to spend time alone with God and develop the discipline of a quiet time. All that I have seen, promote the same elements. Being alone at a designated time (usually they suggest the morning before your day gets started), having a designated area in your home, reading your Bible, writing in a journal about what you have read and how you think the Holy Spirit is encouraging you to apply that to your life, and prayer. The purpose of a quiet time is to spend time alone with God building a personal relationship with Him. The more time you spend with someone, the better you get to know them. The better you know them, the more you trust them! That's what God wants us to do, trust Him! Nothing compares to abiding in HIM and HIS Word.

Hopefully you have already established that precious time with HIM. It is the best decision you could ever make. I wish I could provide you with the place, the prayers, the journal, and the desire. I cannot. I can, however provide you with some scripture to read when you decide to go. We will explore some scriptures together today on the subject of trust. We won't have time to explore them all today, so I will list additional scriptures at the end of this lesson for you to go back to when you have your quiet time!

1) Let's read Proverbs 3:5-6 and complete the following:

   _____ in the Lord with all your _____; and lean not on

   your own _____. In all your _____ acknowledge Him and He

   _____ direct your paths.

2) What a promise! What does Proverbs 3:5-6 say to you? Write your thoughts on the commands that you are being given and then write what God is promising to do.

3) Read Psalm 118:8 and complete the following:

   It is better to _____ in the Lord than to put confidence in man.

   Can you think of a time when you were disappointed because you put your confidence in man? Write a brief statement about the situation and how it made you feel.

4) Can you think of a time when you trusted God and not man and how that situation turned out? Write a few lines about the situation and how it made you feel.

5) Comparing the two, which situation was best and what lesson comes to mind as you have revisited these two situations?

Finally, we seek security because it gives us a sense of peace. Trusting in ourselves gives us a false sense of security. When we are trusting ourselves, being our own lord, and controlling our own lives, our marriages, our families, etc., the peace that we have is not at all representative of the peace that we have with Christ.

6) Feast on the last verse of scripture we will do together today. Ask yourself if the peace that you have is the peace that is in this promise. Read Isaiah 26:3-4 and complete the following:

Thou wilt keep him in _____ peace, whose _____ is stayed

on thee; because he _____ in thee. _____ in the Lord

forever; for in the Lord Jehovah is _____ strength.

Which one of us does not want perfect peace? There is the security that we all seek. How do we get it? We keep our mind on Him because we trust HIM. When we trust Him, we come to realize that the Lord Jehovah is our everlasting strength! If we would only trust and obey, for there is no other way, to be happy in Jesus, than to trust and obey!

Here are some other scriptures to ponder in your quiet time: Psalm 25:2, 31:6, 55:23, 56:3, 143:8, 37:3, 40:3, 62:8, 115:9, 144:2, Proverbs 28:26, Isaiah 50:10, Jeremiah 49:11, Micah 7:5, Nahum 1:7, Jeremiah 17:5 (there are many others in the Bible - just explore and enjoy!)

Day Three - Obedience Ingredient

Now that we are surrendered, and trust God, the next thing is to obey Him, right? Is that also a part of accepting God's vision for my life? It is the KEY part of it. You see, we can surrender - mentally and in our hearts. We can trust - mentally and in our hearts. But in order for us to obey, we need to act! Obedience is seen. So is disobedience. Let me give you an example. There are two 100 story tall buildings and you are on the roof of one of them. The one you are on is burning and will soon be destroyed. If you don't do anything different, you will be destroyed with the building. There is a bridge between the two buildings - a two by four board - not nailed down. Your best friend, whom you adore and have always wanted to be just like, whom you trust with your life, is safely standing on the other roof. He is calling to you to trust him and walk across the two by four to safety. If I were to ask you can you surrender to his will for you to walk to safety, you would say yes. If I were to ask you if you trust him, you would answer yes. If I were to say to you "walk across the board" and you did, that is obedience. If you didn't, that is disobedience. Just like we wouldn't get to safety if we did not obey in the example given, neither will we realize God's vision for our lives without the obedience ingredient.

As we read yesterday in Isaiah 26:3-4, perfect peace - the promise of it and the realty lived gives us the strength everlasting. Does it come automatically? NO! It is something just like surrender and trust, we have to work on daily. Can you see it is a building process? The more we surrender the more open we are to trusting Him with all our care. The more we trust Him with our lives, the more apt we are to be obedient to His commands. So how does one learn to be obedient? One day, one act at a time. What is a tangible act of obedience I can apply to my marriage right now that God will bless? I'll give you one and then a follow up that you might need if this doesn't go like planned!

Assuming you and your spouse spend the majority of the daytime hours apart, when you see each other tonight, greet each other with a hug and a friendly kiss. Sit down for ten minutes and listen to each other tell about their day - no judging, just a friendly ear. That is being compassionate and sympathetic to each other and putting your spouse's needs above yours. That is treating each other with brotherly/sisterly love and being courteous - as courteous, I might add, as you would be to a houseguest who had been out all day! These instructions on how to treat each other are directed right to the husband and wife in 1 Peter 3:8. If you get angry when your spouse doesn't return the gesture with the same degree of brotherly/sisterly love and courtesy, then your follow up act of obedience will be in giving a "soft answer" if your feelings are hurt. Instead of returning "evil for evil" at that point (1 Peter 3:9), hit him/her with a Proverbs 15:1 - "a soft answer turns away wrath!" You might be thinking, "I'm the one that will be mad, my spouse will be the one laughing!" It doesn't matter, Proverbs 15:1 works both ways! If you are the one angry, and you still obey and give a soft answer to her reaction, the soft answer will defuse your anger. You know why? God blesses obedience! How will God bless that obedience?

You keep doing this scenario over and over again and eventually it will become natural to treat your spouse with kindness! I have no idea how he/she will react over time, but I know how much good it will do your heart! By the way, it works well with children too. If your home is one where there are not too many kind words spoken between the occupants, purpose in your heart to speak that way, always, and see what happens. You just go around Proverb 16:24ing them and see what happens!

1) Complete the following from Proverbs 16:24.

_____ words are as an honeycomb, _____ to the soul, and _____ to the bones!

Pleasant words! They are sweet to everyone's soul (including your family members!) and health to everyone's bones!

This example is just one act of obedience to a few different scriptures. I want us to take a look at two examples of people in the Bible that were given something to do by God. Do not think of them as being any different than you, as they were just as human as you and I are. They had a choice just like you and I do to obey or not. First, let's look at a couple by the name of Ananias and Sapphira. Read Acts 4:32 through Acts 5:1-11.

2) What were they supposed to do?

3) What did they do?

4) What happened to them?

5) Did they realize Gods vision for their lives? Explain.

Now let's look at Jesus. You say, wait a minute! Jesus was God! Of course He was obedient! Well, as Christians, we believe that while Jesus was fully God, He was also fully human. Doesn't that mean He had a choice too? Scripture says He was tempted just like we are. Jesus came to earth not only to teach us about the Kingdom of Heaven, but to provide the way for us to get there, by dying for our sins. He was the sacrificial lamb. God the Father sent Him to earth. He knew what He had to do. We are going to pick up the scriptures at Matthew 26:36- 42.

6) Concentrating on the struggle Jesus was experiencing, look at verse 38. How did Jesus describe his soul?

7) In verse 39, What did Jesus pray to His Father?

8) In verse 42, What did Jesus pray to His Father?

9) Go to verses 53, 54, and 56. What does Jesus say about the fulfillment of scriptures?

10) As we know, Jesus was crucified and arose on the third day, just like the scriptures prophesied. Read Matthew 28:18. Did Jesus realize God's vision for Him? Explain.

11) What did Jesus tell everybody to do (that includes us too you know!) in verses 19 and 20?

Call me crazy, but I believe "all those things He commanded us to do" start in our own home with our own spouse and children. Friend, when we get it right in our homes, the rest is a piece of cake! When our hearts are right, our homes reflect that. If our homes, churches, communities, states, and nations were to surrender our hearts to God, what would this world look like? Are you getting the picture? Would getting our hearts right in our own homes allow us to realize God's vision for our lives? You bet! Giving the example, it wouldn't just benefit our own homes, rather the whole world. Changing laws won't do it. Making laws won't do it. God knew that. He gave His people the Law - they were still in a mess! Hearts have to change.

Changed hearts = changed lives. I could spend my time changing laws and making new ones. I do what I can to advocate the ones I believe in. But friend, just like God knew before the foundations of the earth, it wasn't the Law that was going to save mankind. It was a heart filled with the love of Christ and dedicated to His service and Lordship. Jesus is the salvation of the world. Without that relationship, without our obedience to His commandments, without our knowledge, understanding, and application of His Word, (which is His will) we will not realize God's vision for our lives. As we close today, I want us to think about two things:

12) What would your life be like if Jesus had not have been obedient to His Father's will?

13) What would your life, marriage, family be like if you were obedient to the Fathers will?

Take additional time and record more thoughts in your journal.

Day Four – The "As Is" spouse and God's vision

We are going to talk about our spouses today. Life is a process isn't it? Growing spiritually is a process. Growing in God's truth is a process. Becoming who God created us to be is a process. Part of the process of becoming rooted and grounded in our faith is accepting (receiving willingly) God's Word as the truth by which we live. What happens when we, as individuals, choose to live that way, but our spouse does not? Can we still realize God's vision for our lives? We talked about this some in Week Five - Day Five. I would encourage you to go back to that lesson right now and refresh your memory with the things we shared and any notes you may have made.

It is not likely that you both will make changes together - at least in the beginning - and possibly never. The important part to understand is that as much as this is a process for you, it is also a process for your spouse. Rarely do I see a couple make this decision and then grow at the same pace. So what do you do? Learn patience, long-suffering, kindness, etc. - Galatians 5:22 talks about the fruit of the spirit being love, joy, peace, long-suffering, gentleness, goodness, faith, meekness, temperance (self-control) - and it says against such, there is no law! See? No blame can be placed on the person who walks in the spirit and has the manifestation of the fruit in their lives. Your spouse is what he/she is! You cannot change another person. You have control over one person my friend and that is you! Does God have a vision for your spouse? Yes. Can you live God's vision for you even though your spouse is not living out his or hers? YES!

If you started affirming each other as God created you to be, what do you think would happen? A great way to do that is in prayer, together! Most Christian couples I meet do not pray together. What a blessing is missed when you don't pray together. I know it might be uncomfortable at first, but in one prayer, the awkwardness would be gone and oh what a blessing awaits you and your family. When we pray with each other, we get to hear each other's heart. Praying together and praying scripture is a great way to start moving towards that biblical view for your marriage, family order, and home. As you pray together, you could let each other hear you thank God for the order of family and ask HIM to start bringing that order to your home. If you are not praying together, start today! He knows where we are and what HE HAS TO DO TO GET US WHERE HE WANTS US! It goes back to trusting God with all our heart and leaning not on our own understanding (or strength) rather in all our ways acknowledging Him and (believing that) He will direct our paths!

A complaint I hear often is "I just wish he or she would be what God wants him or her to be!" You might be different, but what that really means (I have come to learn) is you want God to want your spouse to be what you want your spouse to be! Let me give you two examples, one for the benefit of both sexes. First example is for the ladies. Suppose all of a sudden your husband came home and said "honey, I heard from God today! We are selling the house, moving to a village in Africa and spending the rest of our lives being missionaries!" Would you say "I'll get the REALTY company on the phone" or would you say "you need a REALITY check?" Guys what would you say if she came home and said "I heard from God today. He told me you are the head of the household and the provider of the family so I quit my job. Here's the checkbook and the bills. We have $100 until payday - next week!" Would you jump for joy? I find we really don't know what we want each other to be because we don't know what we are supposed to look like. We spend too much time looking in the wrong place. It doesn't start with us. It starts with God, His Word, His World, His Ways, His Will.

There is a solution. It is in the person Jesus Christ. He is the way the truth and the life! It doesn't happen overnight, but it does happen, one obedient step at a time. I know you are thinking I tricked you. You thought when I said we were going to talk about our spouses today it meant we were going to sock it to them! It wasn't meant to be a trick. We have to accept our spouses as they are. We have to seek our identity in Christ and so does our spouse. It is a great idea to know what your spouse's identity looks like according to God's Word. Not so you can beat them up with vicious words and accusations of wrongdoings, rather so we can support each other with words of encouragement and prayer. Will your obedience rub off on them, sanctify them, or cause them to obey the word? According to scripture it will! Let's look at some scripture that backs this up:

1) Read 1 Corinthians 7: 14 and complete the following:

For the _____ husband is sanctified by the _____; and the

_____ wife is sanctified by the husband; else were your

_____ unclean; but now they are holy!

2) What does that mean to you?

3) Read 1st Peter 3:1 and complete the following:

Likewise, ye wives, be in subjection to your _____ husbands; that, if any

_____ not obey the _____, they also may, without a word, be won by the

conduct of their wives!

Wait a minute! You mean that if a wife is subject to her own husband, (and we will talk about what that means in week ten), that even if he does not obey the WORD, he will without a word (from her!) be won by her conversation and conduct? That's what the Bible says! I put it to the test and the blessings have been immeasurable! Ray does read the Word now! I am not boasting in anything other than the hope that I have found in Christ Jesus.

As wonderful as all of that is, and as grateful as Ray and I both are that both of us love the Lord, my reward before it all changed was found in the Lord Jesus Christ, and our reward after it all changed, is still found in the Lord Jesus Christ. That's what I mean when I say we can't start with each other we have to each start with the Lord. Why? Let's look at Colossians 3:23-24. Read it and complete the following:

4) And _____ you do, do it heartily as to the _____, and not

    to men; knowing that from the Lord you will receive the _____ of the

    inheritance; for you serve the Lord Christ.

Our reward comes from God! It does not come from our spouse. They cannot, as much as they might even want to, reward us with the things that only God can reward us with. It is not within their power. That power and gift and blessing belongs to God. I had to learn to stop looking to Ray for the things that only God could grant. I thought it was noble to love God and depend on Ray, until God showed me that He wanted me to love Ray and depend on God! I had it backwards! I know that some of you are ready to try this, and there may be others that this is just too "over the top" for right now. The thing I want you to get from today's lesson is this. Your spouse is "as is." God has a vision for him/her (in addition to surrendering self, trusting, and obeying.) Study that vision by meditating on the verses at the end of this section. Ask God to teach you how to start living that vision.

Scriptures to study: Genesis 2:18-25, Ephesians 5:21-33, 1Peter 3:7. As you begin to believe and live this vision, so will your spouse. Record your thoughts in your journal.

Day Five - Faith

It has been a wonderful week hasn't it? The vision that God has for you is the same vision He has for all of His children. He wants us to surrender ourselves to His Lordship, trust Him with all our heart, and obey Him in all that we do. We each as men and women have different roles and responsibilities. I used to go into the different roles as I taught this class, but as the years have gone by, I sense it is best to point to scripture and allow the Holy Spirit to work out the manifestation of those roles.

Surrender, trust, obedience, and faith have no gender. It is through the surrender, trust, obedience, and faith that the roles and responsibilities will be revealed. Culture provides us with a world view of our roles. Cultural world view and Biblical world view are two different things. Knowing who is supposed to do what is not nearly as important as is developing an environment of love and respect. If I find out I am supposed to do the cooking, the cleaning, and the laundry, and he gets to control the money, I might not be too happy if we have missed the environment of love and respect where we all work together to bring honor and glory to God in our marriages and homes. Just as a matter of clarification, I don't think it really matters who does the cooking cleaning and laundry, those are not necessarily the "roles" or "responsibilities" I am talking about seeking the Lord in.

Faith is the substance of things hoped for and the evidence of things not seen. (Hebrews 11:1) The great chapter of faith, as some refer to it, is found in Hebrews 11. What can we do apart from faith? Oh friends. It is our faith that allows us to surrender, trust, obey, and believe that the substance of the things we hope for will one day be seen. How could we even be Christians if it weren't for faith? Which one of us has seen Jesus? Which one of us was there when Mary conceived or gave birth? Which one of us was there when Jesus was crucified and rose again on the third day? None of us..........it is our faith that pleases God and it is impossible to please HIM without faith. If Jesus wasn't born of the Virgin Mary, He did not resurrect. These are the foundational truths of our Christian beliefs. If He did not resurrect, He is not sitting at the right hand of God, and the Word that Jesus became is not a living Word. If it is not a living Word, it will not work. It is a living Word and He lives in us through His Holy Spirit.

1) Read Hebrews 11:6 and complete the following:

But without _____ it is impossible to please Him, for he who comes to God

must _____ that He is, and that He is a _____ of those who

diligently seek Him.

Without faith it is impossible to please God. For those that come to Him must believe that He is - that He is what? That He is God! And God is a (the) rewarder of those who diligently seek Him. Does it say He rewards some of those who diligently seek Him? No! It says He is the rewarder of those, anyone, all of those, who diligently seek Him. Friend I am wanting that reward! You mean I can live in a home where my husband loves me and is the head of our family? I can love and respect him? The environment in our home can be that of love, patience, kindness, gentleness, joy, faithfulness, goodness, peace, and self-control (by everyone?). That's exactly what I mean! I have faith that if I surrender to God, trust in Him, and obey his commands, He will reward us with the goodness He wants us to know in our family. I can assure you that my family has been rewarded time and time again with His goodness and blessings. Are we totally 100% where God wants us to be? No, but we continue to try and diligently seek Him.

Let me give you an example of something we practice in our home that might shed some light on this subject. As of this writing, our son is 24 years old. We have taught him from the earliest days to always be thankful to God for everything, even the bad things. He has, to date, always demonstrated that practice. If he has ever shown an attitude of "that's not fair" he has not done so around me. Not because I told him he couldn't, and not because he hasn't ever been disappointed, rather because my first question to him whenever something bad happens is "have you thanked God for it yet?" His answer has always been "yes ma'am I have" or "no ma'am I haven't, but I am going to right now." He has been taught that as Christians, our first reaction to everything is one of thanksgiving. We believe that to thank God for everything is to practice Philippians 4:6-7. Read that and complete the following:

2) Be _____ for nothing, but in all things, through prayer and supplication,

with _____, let your requests be made known unto God, and the

_____ of God, which passes all understanding, shall keep your _____

and _____ through Christ Jesus.

What have the rewards of that been? Our relationship with our son has always been one of peace. Yes we have had disagreements through the years, but for the most part, they have been handled with respect. We have never had a shouting match like I have heard and heard of with other people and their teenagers (or younger children for that matter). I know all of that could change tomorrow, but to date, I believe God has blessed our home with that type of peace and respect. Not because we are lucky, but because we have sought to apply that command to our lives. When Jesus is keeping our hearts and our minds through Him, peace is promised. When the peace of God prevails so do cool calm heads and hearts. I share that story with you not to exalt my family, rather to give testimony to the word of God. God's word is alive!

3) The message I want us to end this week with is this: Faith without works is dead! People will know our faith by our works. Let's look at James 2:17-20 and complete the following:

Thus also _____, by itself, if it does not have works, is

_____. But someone will say, "You have _____, and I have

_____." Show me your _____ without your

_____, and I will show you my _____ by my

works! You believe that there is one God? You do well. Even the demons _____,

and tremble! But do you want to know oh foolish man, that _____

without _____ is dead!

It is not enough for us just to believe that Jesus lived. It is not enough for us to just call ourselves Christians. Our works should be a testimony of our faith. You want to know something? Our works are a testimony of our faith! For some of us that is good but for some of us that is scary! What goes on inside your home? Guess what? It doesn't stay there. People outside our homes can see it whether we want them to or not. Friend, as we now live in a world where same sex marriage is celebrated, where divorce is running rampant, where children are born out of wedlock by the hour, and where living together is an acceptable arrangement, **WE BETTER GET SERIOUS ABOUT OUR MARRIAGES!** The Christian marriage has got to be the light! The Christian marriage has got to be the salt! When we make those sarcastic little comments about our spouse, when we aren't all that God calls us to be in our homes that is salt losing its flavor! That is hiding our light under a basket.

4) Lets read Matthew 5:13-16 and complete the following:

You are the _____ of the earth; but if the salt _____ its

flavor, how shall it be seasoned? It is then good for nothing but to be

_____ out and trampled under the _____ of men. You are

the _____ of the world. A city that is set on a hill cannot be hidden. Nor do

they _____ a lamp and put it under a _____ but on a lamp stand

and it gives _____ to all who are in the house. Let your _____ so

shine before men, that they may see your _____ works and glorify your

_____ in heaven.

Do we want the salt to lose its flavor? Do we want the light to be put under a basket? I am afraid that is exactly what we have done in the church. That is why divorce for the Christian is no different statistically than it is for the world. Let me tell you where it starts. We are great at playing Christian when all it requires of us is to do things at church and be nice to the people there. However, we are horrible at home! If we were to ask for a show of hands this Sunday in church of all the people who start their day in the Word, or spend any part of the day in the Word, it would be embarrassing. That's why it is hard to tell the church from the world. That's why our marriages and homes are in shambles. Being a Christian is not making a difference in our homes, because we are not spending time learning how to be Christians in our homes. We will never realize Gods vision for our lives if we are not spending time with Him allowing Him to teach us how to surrender, trust, obey, and live out our faith.

In this world where there is so much dysfunction and digression in the American family unit, our lives, marriages, families and homes should be beacons of light and pillars of salt! It is not okay that we tear our spouses down and dishonor them. It is not okay that they do that to us. It is not okay that we disregard the commands of God where the conduct in our homes goes undisciplined. It is not the world that God will hold accountable. It is His people who lost its flavor and hid its light. It is you and me. As we come to a close for this week, please reflect on the things we have learned and go to God in prayer. Start talking to Him about surrender, trust, obedience, and faith. I constantly have to remind myself I am salt and light and it is a responsibility I was charged with when I became a Christian. To take His name, is to take His light. Let it shine! Let it shine! Will you make the decision to accept God's vision for your life?

Record your thoughts in your journal.

WEEK
Nine
Priorities

If you have surrendered to God's vision for your life, congratulations. As you surrender, trust, obey, and start living out your faith, God will reveal the most important things for you to focus on. Those things will become your priorities.

I worked for a bank for eight years. For the last three of those eight years, I worked in an extremely verbally and emotionally abusive situation. Fearful of losing that almighty paycheck I put up with the verbal and emotional abuse for much longer than I should have. Finally, I grew to a point in my faith where I trusted God more than I trusted the paycheck. Ray and I agreed it was time for me to resign. I will never forget that day. When I came home after delivering my resignation letter, I literally fell into my "quiet time" chair. The position of that chair in my living room allowed me to face my front door. As I sat staring at that door in an emotionally and physically drained state, I made a promise to God. I said "God, I will never again go out of that door for a job, a career, a position at church, or do anything that you do not totally 100% lead me to do! I was exhausted. Can any of you relate to that?

For years Ray had been telling me that I put everything and everybody before him. He was right! Our relationship did not hold first place in my heart. Other things were more important to me. I was 36 years old, a wife, a mother, sister, friend, (co-worker up to that point!), on several committees at church, very involved in missions activities, etc. etc. I was so busy and very tired. Everything was out of balance. The thing that puzzled me most was how I could be a Christian, serve God in all the ways I did, yet be so tired and miserable? Where was the joy and why was my life such a wreck? Having just resigned from my job, I had plenty of time to figure all of that out. I am going to share with you exactly how God stilled my soul, renewed my spirit, and directed my steps to live a more peaceful life.

Day One - Why do I have to do it all?

It is a funny thing about women. Rarely do I meet one who doesn't think she does it all. Maybe she does. Guys, let me give you some insight. It has been my observation that for most women, our priority is to just make it through the day. If it is Monday, we wake up to an alarm, wake up the rest of the household, see to it everyone is dressed in something clean, fed, and shoved out the door. We do whatever it is we do (either work outside the home or inside the home) while everybody else is doing whatever they do. Then it's back home again for dinner... for them. For her it is time to cook the dinner and clean up. Depending on your life stage, you might have school aged children that need to do homework, have baths, and need to get ready for bed - or your children are grown and you have lived past that familiar situation - or you have preschoolers and daycare situations. You might have a meeting at church or some other "worthy" work that needs to be done. Finally around 10:00 or 11:00 you can start thinking about bed, if of course the laundry has been done! Oh! Wait a minute! You haven't spent any quality time with your husband. He might even remind you of that. That's when it all explodes! You start re-capping your day! After five minutes, he's sorry he asked! You both go to bed mad. Not to worry though, tomorrow is Tuesday!

Now on Tuesday, you wake up to an alarm clock, wake up the rest of the household, see to it everyone is dressed in something clean, fed, and shoved out the door. You do whatever you do, while everybody else is off doing whatever they do and ... wait a minute. That sounds like Monday! It also sounds like Wednesday, Thursday, and Friday. Saturday is a little different because you get to clean the whole house, do the rest of the laundry, go to the grocery store, put the groceries away, feed everybody, and get the clothes pressed and laid out for church tomorrow morning! Maybe, in between all of that, you have been to a soccer game and a birthday party.

We run ourselves ragged don't we? While all, or at least many, of the things we fill our days with might seem to be "good" they are not necessarily of or from God. Our lives cannot bring glory to God when we are strung out on "overload!" I see it in so many women. They have the "I have to do it all" look on their face. The truth is they might be doing it all. Many women have the responsibility of running their household. Whether they volunteer for it, or get stuck with it makes no difference. The result is the same. Obviously this is written from a woman's point of view. It is possible that the man handles some or all of these responsibilities. Regardless of who handles them, they leave the person very tired and overwhelmed. These are just the basics of running a household and family and it takes the husband and wife working together to do it all successfully. It should not be a burden on one person. Young families today are so busy. It is no wonder so many couples and families are at each other's throats. It's not because you don't love each other, it's because you're worn out trying to get everything done! Our lifestyles represent anything but peace, yet God wants to give us peace. He wants us to be still enough to hear HIM. We can't hear HIM when our lives are going 100 miles a minute, every minute of the day. So how do you change it all? Glad you asked ...

I know you are familiar with the story of Mary and Martha in the Bible. Martha was busy "doing" while Mary was sitting at the feet of Jesus, listening to the Master teach. Martha got so irritated that she told Jesus to tell Mary to come in the kitchen and help her! Jesus did just the opposite! He told Martha that she worried about many things and that Mary, in fact, had chosen the best part! I can hear Martha now. "Well if that doesn't beat all. Here I am kind enough to invite these people into my house, serve refreshments, and make things hospitable for them. I am serving my Lord and doing this work for Him and His friends. All I want is some help, and even God tells me I am worrying too much and what Mary is doing is better than what I am doing!" It just doesn't seem right does it? Serving the Lord, and yet the Lord says "what you are doing is not the best part." We need to explore that.

1)   Read Luke 10: 38-42

     Martha "welcomed" Jesus and those he was traveling with into her home. What has to take place in your home for you to feel comfortable entertaining guests?

2)   What is your mood when you have prepared your home for guests and your spouse and children are not helping?

3) Do you think Martha was mad at Mary? Explain your answer.

4) What do you think Jesus was really teaching Martha?

5) What are you learning from this?

I began to learn that just because something was important to me it didn't mean it was important to anyone else. If keeping the house prepared for guests is important to me, that's okay but it doesn't necessarily mean it is important to anyone else in my house. Yelling and fussing at my family before the guests arrive because they "never help me" and being mad at them after the guests leave, for the same reason, means that I am the one off balanced. Whatever "serving" went on when the guests were there could not possibly override or undo the damage that was done to the hearts and minds of my loved ones. The truth is our homes should be routinely maintained to the entire family's comfort level. All of the members of the family should be concerned with that maintenance. It used to be I would only clean if we had company coming over. That says two things to me, about me. One, I valued outsiders opinions more than my own family and two, I should think my own family was worthy of a clean house whether we had company or not. Now, I keep the house to our satisfaction. If company likes it, great! If not, it doesn't bother me.

The first thing we need to learn about priorities is how to determine what is important and what is not. I am just using the example of a clean house. There are many other things on our agendas we could talk about. We have lots to do in our busy lives, and we need to learn how to prioritize them according to God - not us.

6) Going back to the example with Martha and Mary, what did Jesus tell Martha in verses 41 and 42?

7) He told her that only one thing is needed and Mary had chosen that good part. What was the good part that Mary had chosen?

8) Why do you think Jesus said that was the good part?

9) If you chose the "one thing needed" the "good part" how do you think that would affect you and your family?

Spend the remainder of your quiet time today writing in your journal about the things you have to do to run your household and make sure your family and all of your other obligations run smoothly. Tomorrow we are going to examine our schedules more closely. The list needs to be fresh on your mind! Ask God to impress upon you the importance of the things you write down.

Day Two – What (or who) are my priorities?

Do you (we) prioritize things or people? That is an interesting question isn't it? What should we prioritize? What does the word even mean? Webster's New World Dictionary defines "prioritize" in this way: to arrange in order of importance. That is a fair definition I think. With that definition in mind, let's be honest about how we arrange our days. For most of us, I suppose, Monday through Friday are pretty much the same. Using the table below, sketch out your week.

Time of Day	Monday	Tuesday	Wednesday	Thursday	Friday
5:00 am					
6:00 am					
7:00 am					
8:00 am					
9:00am					
10:00am					
11:00am					
12:00pm					
1:00pm					
2:00pm					
3:00pm					
4:00pm					
5:00pm					
6:00pm					
7:00pm					
8:00pm					
9:00pm					
10:00pm					
11:00pm					
12:00am					

Now, write out your typical Saturday and Sunday routines below:

Time of Day	Saturday	Sunday

1) Based on the charts you just filled out, what and who are your priorities?

I have done this exercise many times over the last fifteen years. It is very revealing isn't it? It is a great tool to use to figure out several things. For instance, it will show how productive, or, as the case may be, non-productive our days are. Are your days filled with "busy" work? How much wasted time is in your schedule? Does it show you are confusing activity with accomplishment? What does it reveal to you about the importance of the people and relationships in your life? It will most definitely show how important we think it is to spend time alone with God ... uh oh! Go back to the schedule. Are there any time slots dedicated to sitting at the feet of Jesus? Is having a quiet time with prayer and Bible study in your daily schedule?

Today is a short lesson. Spend the remainder of your time this morning studying your schedule and asking God to prepare your heart for how you can better prioritize not just your schedule, but your whole life. You have made the decision to accept God's vision for your life. He has to be the priority. He has to be first. We will never truly know HIM or live His vision, if he is not first. To help with the preparation of our hearts this morning, read Exodus 20:3.

2) Write out that commandment.

If we are to have no other gods before our God, read over your schedule and start allowing the Holy Spirit of truth to reveal areas that could possibly be in violation of that command. Tomorrow we will determine what in our lives are of God and what is not.

Day Three - Is it God? Or is it me?

If we are really serious about living our lives for God, if we are really serious about accepting His vision for our lives, we will want to get rid of the things in our lives that are not of or from Him. I am not talking about walking up to your boss and saying "God wants me to quit!" Nor am I suggesting you need to call your pastor and tell him that you are resigning your positions at church. What I am suggesting is that it is vital to assess how we spend our time. IF GOD DID NOT CALL YOU TO IT, YOU DON'T WANT TO DO IT!

When Ray and I started going to our church, the pastor offered some very wise, sound advice. He came to visit us just after we joined the church and he suggested that we would probably be asked to participate in all kinds of programs and maybe even to serve on some committees. After all, we were a young married couple, no children at the time, so we were prime targets with all of that time and energy on our hands. His advice to us was to make sure we did NOT say yes to anything right away. In fact, he encouraged us to just come to church for a while and really prayerfully consider where God might have us serve before we just jumped right into a position. Did we listen? Absolutely not! Within no time, we were working with the youth. Within six months I was starting (not just participating mind you, no, I was leading!) a woman's mission group for women ages 18 to 35. I joined the choir, signed up for nursery work, and helped with the teenage girl's mission group. We were at church Sunday morning, Sunday evening, Wednesday evening, Thursday for choir practice, and some Tuesday's for visitation.

It was a great time ... for a while. After five years of it, I was exhausted, Ray was feeling neglected. We had been blessed with our little guy during that time, so he was feeling the wounds too.

Between work, church, and motherhood, I was simply, no good! Notice, I didn't even say anything about being a wife. We were roommates at best! We barely spoke to each other. The extent of our conversations revolved around who was picking Mark up from daycare and what we were having for dinner! I finally reached the end of my rope. I was tired. I could not handle my life anymore. I could not handle my schedule anymore. I was weak and didn't care who knew it. So in the middle of my living room floor, I cried ... and cried ... and cried. I could not stop nor could I tell Ray why I was even crying. I didn't know. I know now.

My life was so out of balance. The good news is I had maintained a daily quiet time with God for the previous 11 years. I was broken. I had finally fallen on my knees before God Almighty, asking Him in desperation to fix whatever it was that was ailing me. He knew I was ready to surrender whatever I needed to Him. Sometimes God has to get me in a special position in order for me to hear Him. He had my attention. He started showing me why my life was such an abomination to me. It was an abomination to Him.

1)   Read Proverbs 11:1. Write it.

2)   What does that say to you?

It spoke to me loud and clear. Some versions say "dishonest scales", some say "a false balance" is an abomination to the Lord. My life was very much off balance. When I realized my life being out of balance was not only an abomination to me, but to God too, I asked Him to show me how to change my life so it honored HIM. He had me do the same exercise we did yesterday. That gave me a great understanding of why I was so miserable. Every minute of every day was full. Even if it was full of TV, it was full. It was not that I was doing anything bad. In fact they were good things. They just weren't necessarily from God. There is a big difference in doing something good - even if it is godly- and doing something God has called you to do. One is perfect, the other can be permissive, and it can even be disobedient if done for any other reason than God led you to it.

Suppose Jesus came to earth and did everything he did except go to the cross? Suppose when it came time to go to the cross, Jesus said "Father, I just can't do that, so I think I'll stay here and start a church and watch it grow." That might have been good, but would it have been God's perfect will? No. God's perfect will was for Jesus to be the sacrificial lamb that would save those who believe in HIM and to conquer sin and death. Jesus would be the only one who could reconcile the lost with the Father because no one comes to the Father except through the Son (John 14:6). Jesus lived His life according to God's will. We need to do the same.

3)   Read Proverbs 16:3 and write it below.

Commit your works to the Lord and your thoughts will be established! Wow. What a promise. Is it really that simple? Yes! It is. Simple yes, easy not necessarily. Go back to the schedule you wrote out yesterday. Spend the remainder of your time today committing all of that to the Lord. All of that is considered your work. If you work outside or inside the home, it doesn't matter. Your work is not just limited to your 9 to 5 job. Our work involves all that we do. Whether we are being paid for it or not, is irrelevant. Commit all that you do to the Lord, and He will establish your thoughts. In other words, He will let us know if we need to be doing it or not. Commit that schedule to Him and then listen to the thoughts He will begin establishing. You will find out real quick if it is of you, or if it is of God, what's important and what is not.

Day Four - Purge and Purify

Perhaps all you can see is this big mess you've gotten yourself into and now you are wondering how you are going to get out of it. After all, you can't just stop this merry-go-round of life. You still have work to do inside and/or outside of the home. You still have a family that has needs. You still have the commitments. You can't just run away and hide. But you can allow God to purge and purify your life. What does that mean?

To purge, means to get rid of something. To purify, means to be cleansed of all impurities. This will not happen overnight. It is a process. As God started encouraging me to pay close attention to the way I spent my time, He impressed upon my heart that I needed to free up my schedule. He also let me know that as my schedule was freed up, I was not to replace the time slots with anything else. I thought that was strange! As much as we complain about our full schedules, in an odd sort of way, it is our comfort zone. What I came to learn, however, was as my time became more and more uncommitted, I had more time to spend with God. The more time I spent with Him, the better my relationship became with my husband and son. The more relaxed I became, the more organized my home became and things ran much smoother. Is this making any sense? We were enjoying family life! We were actually at home, satisfied not to go anywhere. We were spending time at the end of the work day, at home with one another, laughing and talking. We were even relaxed! Guess what I learned? If you are going to be a family, you have to be a family at home! If you are going to have a home, instead of just a house where everyone sleeps at night, you have to spend time at home!

Eventually, God purged me from every commitment I had, outside of the home. He allowed me time at home, alone and with my family. We all grew to love it, and we grew from it, as a family of God. We could have allowed the pressure of going from two incomes to one all of a sudden, really scare or rush us back into the same situation. We did not. We believed God wanted me home. It did not take long to start realizing the benefits of having me home. That might not be what God would have for your family. It was unquestionably what He had for ours. I had to contribute to the household income. He provided a way for me to do that without being away from my family. Eventually, God led me to work for my husband. I would have laughed at that idea 10 years earlier. When we were obedient to God He led us to His plan for our family. All of what we went through, and still go through, in my opinion, is to constantly prepare us for the next step, whatever that may be. God can prepare families to do ministry together, but you first have to become a family, at home. Once the individuals are well, the family becomes well. Once the family becomes well, it can witness to a lost community ... and it might even be the community of believers in your own church He prepares you to witness to.

I don't know what God has in mind for you and your family. I do know that He has an order for the family. Until that order is being followed, the family is not as healthy as God intends it to be. When schedules are so full we do not have a moment to seek God, He will allow us to be broken. That's a good thing. When we are broken, we seek God. When we are so pained by our lives and schedules that we want to get rid of all that we do, God will empty our bags of life. When we are ready, according to Him, He will put the weights back in our bag. Remember yesterday when we looked at Proverbs 11:1 and learned how our out of balanced lives are an abomination to God? Today, we are going to look at Proverbs 16:11 to see what He delights in.

1)   Read and write Proverbs 16:11.

2)   What does that say to you?

In Proverbs 11:1, we learned that a "false balance" or an out of balanced life is an abomination to God, and a "just weight" (balance) is His delight. Proverbs 16:11 tells me that an honest balance belongs to the Lord. When all of the weights in the bag are from God, it is His work, His will that is being done. I wanted all of the weights in my bag (life) to be His! I had reached the point of brokenness that said if God did not want it for me I did not want any part of it. I started living this principle years ago and have not had to be retrained in it ... to date! If I even detect a trace of over commitment, I am right back to examining my schedule and asking God to purge me again! He has taken me through a purge process several times but never as dramatic as the first time. While events leading up to a purge from God can be extremely painful, the rewards from allowing it to happen are immeasurable.

3) If I were to ask you what areas of your life you feel you are overcommitted in, what would you tell me?

4) If I were to ask your husband and children what areas they see you being overcommitted in, what would they tell me? Explain your answer.

5) Do your answers match?   ____ yes ____ no
   If not, why do you think they differ?

Spend the remainder of your time today talking to God and writing in your journal about what a purge process could mean for you and your family. Go back over the schedule you sketched out earlier this week - one more time. Yesterday you were to commit all of your work to God so He could begin to establish your thoughts. Has God started talking to you? Are you sensing God might want to purge your life of some things? Ask God to reveal to you any areas you are overcommitted in. Trust that He will show you the next step. All of this is to point us toward His peace. Tomorrow we will look at the connection between our priorities and God's peace.

Day Five - Priorities/Peace, what's the connection?

Don't we all want peace? I hear so many people (especially women) say "I just want peace in my life." When I ask what that means I usually get similar answers. "I need my life to slow down." "I need my family to stop going in so many directions." "I need to stop being pulled in so many directions." "I need my husband/ wife and children to help out more around the house." It always has something to do with life moving too fast and there being too much to do. God does not call us to that type of life. This entire study has been designed to help us discover God's truths about how we are to generally live our lives, and specifically, how we are to experience God's design for marriage.

We have studied God's truths with regards to our identity as Christian Men and Women, Christian husbands and wives, love, marriage, and family. We know what the Christian home life looks like. We know we have to surrender ourselves to God and we know, in order to live our lives as He would have us live them, we have to accept His vision for our lives. The path, my sweet friends, that leads us from where we are to where He wants us, is the prioritized life. The peace that you, me, and every other man and woman I know seeks, is found when priorities are in alignment with God's priorities (found in His Word). I am not talking about the prioritized list of daily tasks. I am speaking of the priority of relationships and home life. The main relationship of course is our personal relationship with Jesus Christ. I might also add to attain that is not to reach the goal. To attain that only puts us at the start line. To attain that, takes us out of the rat race and puts us in the good race ... God's race, which is the only race worth running.

1) Read and write 2nd Timothy 4:7.

Paul refers to life as the good fight and a race. He was near the end of his life and he was able to say he had fought the good fight, finished the race, and kept the faith. Those are words spoken by a person who was at peace in his heart.

2) Read 2nd Timothy 4:8 and fill in the blanks.

Finally, there is laid up for me the _____ of _____, which the Lord,

the _____ _____, will give to me on that Day, and not

to me only but also to _____ who have loved His appearing.

Paul not only has peace in his heart about how he has lived his life, but he is confident that the life he has led has earned him a crown of righteousness!

Paul was not married, but he had advice (divinely inspired) for those who were. We studied Paul's teachings in Corinthians, Ephesians, and Colossians. When our marriages and homes bear witness to the word of God, not only does that minister to others, it frees us to go out of our homes for ministry. When our homes are healthy, we can teach other families in our church how to become healthy. When our churches are healthy, we have healthy communities. When God's people are healthy the world takes note. We try to do it backwards. It doesn't work. God pours His blessings from the top down and when those blessings are running over, they are running out to others in the world. When Ray and I are properly aligned inside the will and word of God, there is nothing to block those blessings. We receive them, our son receives them, our extended family receives them, and so does our church family, community, state, nation, and world. Your hope, future, peace, and blessings do not end with this type of lifestyle, it all begins with it.

I shared in Week Eight that in our home, we live with the discipline of thanking God for everything. We do that because that is what is taught in Philippians 4:6-7. It is important enough to repeat.

3) Please read Philippians 4:6-7 and fill in the blanks below.

Be _____ for nothing, but in _____ things, through prayer and

supplication, with THANKSGIVING, make your _____ known unto

God, and the _____ of _____, which passes _____

understanding, shall keep your _____ and _____ through Christ Jesus.

Peace can be described with words like, calm, quiet, harmony, serenity. Anxiety is worry. Peace is freedom from worry. According to the scriptures above, when we catch ourselves in times of anxiety (and all of us are susceptible to it), we are to stop, immediately go into prayer, with thanksgiving, and count on God's peace calming our hearts and our minds through Christ Jesus, so we can then know how to proceed. You say well Jesus is not here to tell me what to do. NO, but His Word is. That's why we have to be studied. That's why we need to sit at His feet daily. That's why we need to be prioritized in our minds according to His word, so we will know what the next step is. That's why we, like Paul, will be able to say I have run the race and kept the faith. Which one of us does not want to have that assurance, that peace in our hearts about how we have lived our lives?

That is the connection between priorities and peace. Paul didn't have to be prioritized in his marriage because he wasn't married. But he knew the importance of married couples being prioritized in their relationships with one another and their children. When we live inside of God's Kingdom, we do things God's way. We will not know God's peace if we do not know God's priorities. Spend the remainder of your time today writing in your journal about anything God is impressing upon your heart to lead you into His peace.

WEEK
Ten

Submission is not a bad word! And it's not just for wives!

How could we get through this study without talking about submission? We could not! Please do not let this section scare you. Contrary to popular secular belief, submission is anything but negative. You may still not agree with it by the time you finish, but you will definitely understand it is not now, nor has it ever been a negative thing. Misinformed users inside and outside of the church have unfortunately taken the subject and distorted its meaning. Many people have linked submission to the Christian wife only. Friends, let me share with you that submission does not begin with the Christian wife. It begins with the Christian. As a Christian, male or female, we submit to the authority of Jesus Christ. Submit, according to the Webster's II New Riverside Dictionary, means to surrender to the authority, discretion, or will of another. We talked a great deal about surrender a couple of weeks ago. We will talk about it more in this lesson.

All authority has been given to Jesus in heaven and on earth according to Matthew 28:18-20. We are to become His disciples, make disciples, and observe and keep all of His commandments. We are to submit, as Christians, to the authority of Jesus Christ. Why are we to do this? God has a Kingdom and He rules. He equips us with all we need to live in that kingdom. As with any kingdom, there is always a ruler. If one is going to live successfully inside the kingdom, one will live in submission to the King or else. As previously stated, the "or else" is never good. God's kingdom is no different. We either submit to His authority, or else, period. Inside His kingdom, He rules! He has a plan for marriage. In God's marriage, He has an order, when successfully followed, assures the followers success. That vision calls for the wife to be subject to her husband's authority which he has been given by God. Husbands are charged with being the head of the wife which is likened unto Christ and the church. It is not a commandment for the man to rule by his fleshly desires or whims, it is a command for the husband to submit himself to the authority of Christ and seek to become to his wife and family what Christ is to the church. Christ demonstrated servant leadership which is the example for men to follow in relation to their families. There is a huge difference between fleshly control and Godly authority.

We have been together for 10 weeks now. No one was more adverse to this submission thing than I was. You have been on the same path God took me on. Because of the journey you have been on over the last couple of weeks, your heart should be prepared to start accepting this. You now know where you started, how you got there, what your false images are, how you got them, and we have explored some of God's truths. You understand God's vision for your life and family and you have accepted His vision as your vision for your life. Your heart should be ready to explore submission, God's way.

I knew I was ready to at least explore submission when God showed me my challenge was not with Ray. I had read too much about "wives being subject to your own husbands" to know that Ray didn't just somehow have that inserted into the text in my personal Bible. I was trusting God enough at that point in my life to know that even though I had a challenge with it, and even though I beat Ray up over it, my feelings and disregard for it, did not change God's order or truth. No matter what truth any of us has a challenge with, it doesn't change the truth. Trust me, Ray would have gladly handed over his place of authority to me if he could have, just to keep the peace! I wouldn't be surprised to learn all husbands would love to be able to change it.

No matter how much either party dislikes it, the truth is the headship is given to the man. It is done by God and God equips man for the position. Women will not be held responsible if the man does not seek God in his role as husband, and men will not be held responsible for the wife who does not seek God in her role as wife. Surrendering to that truth finally allowed me to understand it was much more productive and empowering to explore the wonders of submission. So, off I went on another journey. One that I still have challenges in, but one that has opened up a whole new world for me and a brand new dimension for our marriage.

Day One – What is submission according to God, you, your spouse, the world?

1) If submission means to surrender to the will, discretion, or authority of another person, what do you think God considers submission to be?

All throughout the Bible, we see acts of surrendering to the will, discretion, and authority of God the Father by individuals and even groups of people. For the sake of time, I am going to pick one person whose life we can analyze to help us understand what submission is according to God. We have looked at this briefly in another lesson, it is worth repeating.

2) Read Luke 22:41-44. Jesus was in the garden of Gethsemane the night of His arrest. He knew His time was at hand and He went there to pray to the Father. What did Jesus pray in vs. 42?

3) According to the physical reaction, how painful was it for Jesus to face the cross? (vs. 44)

4) Read Matthew 26:37-38. Jesus began to be sorrowful and deeply distressed. What did He tell his disciples in verse 38?

5) What do you think it means to be exceedingly sorrowful, even unto death?

There are any number of examples I could use in the Bible to demonstrate submission to God's will. I chose this one because Jesus was submissive "even unto death." It is unthinkable that Jesus would have not been submissive to His Father. He asked God to remove "this cup" but in the same breath said "nevertheless not My will, but Yours." Which one of us models that type of submission? Even unto death?

According to God, submission is: 1) understanding that He is the Lord our God and 2) having no other gods before Him. (Exodus 20:2-3) That is how we demonstrate our submission to God. Submission doesn't start in the marriage between husband and wife. Submission starts with the Creator and His created. In the example we used with Jesus, He was totally surrendered to the will of His Father. He wanted that cup to pass from Him. Yet He surrendered to His Father's will. The only way sinful man can stand before Holy God is by being covered in the righteousness of Christ's blood. I don't know why that was God's plan. Those of us blessed with children really cannot begin to comprehend that sacrifice.

6) What does John 3:16 tell us?

7) What does John 3:17 tell us?

You know what I like about that? God was saying "my son is the only one that can save the world!" I have a sticky note on my computer that says "yes, for God so loved the world ... and the son so loved His Father that He fought the darkness with desire to obey!" Jesus loved His Father. He loved us too, but whenever I am tempted to think it was solely Jesus' love for me that He died such a brutal death, I am quickly reminded and humbled to think it was the love for His Father that motivated that ultimate act of love.

8) Read Matthew 28:18. What was the reward for Jesus' submission? What has Jesus been given?

9) Read Philippians 2:9-11.

Who has God the Father highly exalted? _____.

Whose name is above all names? _____.

At the name of Jesus what will all knees do? _____

    what will all tongues confess _____

To whose glory will that be? _____

Jesus has been given all authority in Heaven and Earth and at the very name of Jesus all knees will bow and tongues will confess that Jesus Christ is Lord! He is Lord. There is nothing else! He is the great I AM, the Alpha and Omega, the Beginning and the End. And this is who we serve. This is who we surrender our authority, discretion, and will to. He has a plan and purpose for everything. Inside His plan for marriage there is a healthy order and when it is lived out it creates a healthy environment inside the family. Good things grow inside healthy environments.

The authority He has given to the man to lead the family is a positive factor, not negative like the adversary would have us believe. Just because a man does not recognize or exercise his leadership position as God intends, and just because a woman isn't obedient to the command to submit to her husband, does not mean there is something wrong with God's truth. Nor does it mean the people who think there is something wrong with that truth are less accountable to the command. It is real, it is truth and we are going to be held accountable - male and female.

We do a lot of things routinely that perhaps, at one time, we did not know how to do. One of those things might be driving a car. Before you knew how to drive a car, you probably rode with someone who knew how to drive. You saw people driving cars in movies. You watched people drive cars in your neighborhood. You were always surrounded by people who could drive a car. Until you started driving, however, you did not know how to do it. In fact, until you started driving, you didn't even really know that you could. The ability to drive was always with you, but until you did it, you didn't know that. When you first started, you probably weren't nearly as good as you are now. On the other hand, you might have been more careful in the beginning because you didn't want to mess up. Your driving skills probably resemble the people or person you learned from. Depending on how long you have been driving, you are probably so comfortable with your style and knowledge of driving you no longer look for ways to do it better.

That, my friends, parallels the description of most marriages. We do "marriage" routinely. We imitate the people we learn from. We get our image of marriage and the role's for husbands and wives from movies and sitcoms. We were more careful in the beginning because we didn't want to mess up. Now, we are very comfortable with the style and knowledge we've acquired and we no longer look for ways to make our marriages better.

My point is this. Just because we routinely do marriage, it does not mean we do it right. I have shared with you that the Christian marriage, for the most part, is no different than the "non-Christian" or "worldly" marriage. As I have researched this subject for the last 25+ years, and as I have sought God's Word and attempted to do it God's way, I find there is a huge difference in the two. The world teaches marriage is a 50-50 proposition. The world teaches men and women are the same and that "roles" are basically non-gendered. I believe scripture teaches men and women are equal in relationship to God, but they have different role assignments from God. The remainder of this section will be focused on those roles.

We are going to look at God's plan for submission in the marriage and home.

10) Read Ephesians 5:21.

Who are Christians supposed to submit to? _____

in the fear of who? _____.

11) In Ephesians 5:22, who are wives supposed to submit to? _____ as unto who? _____.

Why? (vs 23) _____.

12) Read vs. 25-33 and write what you think it means and how you think you need to apply it to your life.

The marital relationship is paralleled to Christ and the church. There is an undeniable order. To deny it is to deny the scriptures. I know there are Christians who deny it. I do not know how they can, or why they do. I know there are Christians that say if you believe this way "you don't like women." Is that to say Christ doesn't like the church? No! Christ is the savior of the church. I believe this scripture parallels this as being the man's responsibility to his family. Just as the church is to be subject to Christ, so the wife is to be subject to her own husband. What does that mean? Let's start with the church being subject to Christ. He is the Savior and Lord. The church is to be subject to His authority and His alone ... remember Exodus 20:2-3 - I am the Lord your God ... you shall have no other gods before me. Jesus is the Lord we shall serve. In turn, Jesus is the savior of the church. He does nothing to harm it and everything to save it and prosper it. That is how the two work together. They are one, Christ and the church. Scripture says the parallel is the relationship between husband and wife. Meditating on that truth is how my submission journey began. I must confess that I didn't like it when God starting drawing my heart and mind in alignment with His will on this subject. I thought I was going to lose something if I adhered to this. I agonized. I had to go to the garden alone on this one many times. This meant a huge change for us. Denying it meant disobedience. Disobedience is never good. I stayed and wrestled with God until I could wrestle no more. I surrendered to this truth, and prayed for my Lord to teach me how to live it.

Husbands are to love their wives as Christ loved the church and gave Himself for it. Husbands are to love their wives and wives are to respect their husbands. All of this is representative of God's plan for submission from the church to Christ, and to each other in our families. Submission is not just something women are expected to do. Submission is the Christian Code of Conduct. We are to first submit to God, then to each other in the fear of the Lord. That is what submission is according to God.

13) What is submission according to you?

14) What is submission according to your spouse?

15) What is submission according to the world?

16) What does the definition of submission according to you, your spouse, and the world have in common with God's submission?

17) What source of authority supports your, your spouse's, and the world's definition of submission?

If your answer to the last question is related to emotions, experience, circumstances, tradition, culture, or society, continuing to live according to that source of authority is just going to yield you more of the same heartache you live with now. I know this has been a "heavy" subject to discuss and there has been much to think about. Spend the remainder of your time today writing in your journal and talking to God about this order in your home. Allow the Holy Spirit to guide you into the truth.

Day Two – Understanding the power of submission

God's ways are not our ways and His thoughts are not our thoughts. He doesn't require submission because He wants to be mean, or because He wants us to be miserable.

1) Read John 10:10. Write the words of Jesus.

There is a thief that comes to steal and kill and destroy. Jesus says he comes that we might have life and have it more abundantly. Are you living an abundant life? I am not speaking of abundance of material things. I mean, is your marriage and home life abundantly happy? Are you fulfilled? Is your heart at peace with your marriage, your family, your household? Does your home life depict a lifestyle that you would desire for everybody you know?

That is not to say you are problem free. That is not to say your marriage and family are without challenges. It is to say, for the most part, there is an overwhelming joy in your heart for the life you live. There is a sense of being "settled" and "established" in your marriage and home, and you know your life is what it is because of God. As much as possible you live according to God's ways and you and your family are saved through faith in Christ. You understand the relational order and role assignment for the Christian home and you and everyone in your family lives safely, securely, and abundantly inside of it. Friends, there is not a safer more secure place for a child to be nourished and grow than inside of a home where mom and dad are properly aligned and living as one inside of the order established by Almighty God. There is not a more secure place for a woman to grow than inside the love, protection, understanding, and leadership of a man who loves the Lord and understands his role and position in God. This type of environment frees a man to be the servant leader God has called him to be. This type of environment gives respect to him, love to her, and security to the children. That is the power of submission.

As I started on this submission journey, God allowed my heart to stop focusing on what I thought Ray needed to be or do. He turned my focus toward what His word says about the different roles. As I submitted to the thought of the man and his place in the family, I was encouraged to see Ray in that position. God showed me I just needed to trust HIM and respect the position He had ordained for the husband. By respecting the position and trusting God I began to see Ray in a different light. When my knowledge of who my husband was created to be in God began to grow, my treatment towards him changed.

I started praying for him instead of complaining to God about him. I started praying that image out loud in our prayer time so we both could have the benefit of hearing God's plan. As my treatment towards my husband conformed to God's word, it became natural to respect the position. I totally trusted and submitted to the truth that God knows best. I claimed that Ray was to our family what Christ is to the church. We are still on the journey, but where we are based on where we were, is incredible. The mental freedom that has come with that lifestyle change has made our home a much more honorable place to live. There is a heavy burden a woman shoulders when she seeks to usurp her husband's authority and headship in the family. I also know there is a heavy burden a man feels when he is not submitting to God's authority to lead his family. All of it puts undo stress on the entire family. It is like a thief that comes to rob, steal, and destroy. It cheats the children and stops the flow of blessings. Not to mention the distorted image it then passes onto the next generation. Submitting to God's order for the family structure has created a smooth operation in our home. I believe it has eliminated a ton of emotional garbage our son would otherwise have to carry with him into adulthood and into his marriage. Of course he will have his challenges, and he might not ultimately choose to live like we do. Our picture is not perfect, but I can honestly say I do not know of another family I would trade places with. I hope you feel the same about your home and family life.

2) I have shared two examples of the power of submission. Can you think of a time when you submitted to something God convicted you to do? Explain.

3) What were the results of your submission?

4) What do you think would have happened if you had not been submissive?

Spend the remainder of your time today talking to God about how submission to Him and His ways would equate to an abundant life for you, your marriage, and family.

Day Three - Who do we submit to?

The idea of submission is not foreign to you, you know? In fact, we are all very good at it. That's right. We all not only know how to submit, we already submit ... to someone, even if it is ourselves. It is authority that we buck. We do not like having someone or something telling us what to do. We want to be the masters of our own ships. I will never forget something my mother said to me a long time ago. She said "Robin, you will always have someone you have to answer to. It might be your parents, it might be a boss, a spouse, or God, but you will always have someone you have to answer to." I didn't like that idea then. I understand it now.

Submission really is a simple concept. You give over to the will, discretion, or authority of another person. Parents submit to the will of their children. Employees submit to the will and authority of their employers. Children (sometimes!) submit to the will and authority of their parents. Adults submit to the will of other adults. We all know how to submit to other people.

1) Think of the people and situations in your life you submit to. Listed below are some things/people you might submit to. Put a check beside any that you now, or in the past have submitted to:

__ parents __ boss __ teacher __ coach __ sibling __ child __ pastor

__ counselor __ chairman of a committee __ co-worker __ project leader

__ spouse __ other _____

2) In what ways did you submit to them? (pick a few examples and explain)

3) Was the outcome of your submission positive or negative? Explain.

Depending on the situation, the results of our submission can be positive or negative. For instance, when we give into a source of authority out of selfish reasons (theirs or yours) the results/outcome can be negative. That is never the case with God. Submitting to His authority in our lives will always be blessed because HE always blesses obedience.

I have no problem submitting to the authority of my pastor, who happens to be married. He is another woman's husband. I have had bosses who were married. No problem submitting to them. I have friends who are married. I have no problem submitting to or respecting their husband's position as head of their families. It is a good chance you have no problem with these examples either. So why do women have a problem submitting to our "own" husbands? Is it "the" husband or is it "our own" husband that scripture is more interested in? Is it someone else's husband or your own husband you should be more concerned with?

4) Lets revisit some scripture verses:

Read 1st Peter 3:1. Whose husband are you to be subject to? _____

Read Colossians 3:18. Whose husband are you to be subject to? _____

Read Ephesians 5:22. Whose husband are you to be subject to? _____

Read Titus 2:5. Whose husband are you to be subject to? _____

As a man, you probably have no problem submitting to or respecting another woman. The point here is that we all know how to submit to, be subject to, be respectful to members of the opposite sex. Scripture so beautifully points us to submission as a way to honor our own households and families as they are the ones God has given to us. We cannot have someone else's family. Scripture teaches us how to be holy and happy inside our own lives, within our own marriages, within our own families.

2nd Timothy 3:16-17 says "all scripture is given by inspiration of God and is profitable for doctrine, for reproof, for correction, for instruction in righteousness; that the man of God may be perfect, thoroughly equipped for every good work.." If we believe scripture, we understand the instruction is to bring Glory to God. We reap the benefits of that obedience - which also brings glory to HIM. I believe women are encouraged and commanded to be subject to their own husbands because that is God's plan. It blesses my husband, our marriage, our son and most of all it glorifies God. It doesn't matter what someone else's husband or wife does, or is, or becomes. My eyes, respect, submission and allegiance belong to my husband. Obedience to that for me yields great rewards for my marriage and my family. You can't have someone else's husband or wife. Giving preference to your own husband or wife, in your own family, in your own home starts making your own situation special. So often we break the tenth commandment by coveting what our neighbors have, thinking "if only my wife would be like Rick's wife."

My suggestion is, go talk to Rick. He'll more than likely give you the real scoop. Then you will realize you have wasted a lot of time wishing for something Rick doesn't have either! It is all part of the great deception by the thief, the robber, the destroyer who doesn't want us to have an abundant life. The destroyer wants us to keep our eyes off of the gifts God has given us in our own spouse, and covet what we perceive the lives of others to be. NO. NO. NO. Accept your own spouse as a gift from God. It doesn't mean you won't get on each other's nerves. It doesn't mean there won't be disagreements. It means you are special to and for each other, and as you honor each other the less important the irritants will be.

Focus on your own home. Allow God to have His way with your own heart. He created the order. Trust that it is for HIS Glory and pursue it. You and your family will benefit tremendously from doing that. Spend the remainder of your time today writing in your journal about ways God might be leading you to submit to your "own" spouse. (Ephesians 5:21) Think of what your marriage and home life could be. Ponder the fact that God wants to bless your marriage. Write your thoughts.

Day Four – Submission: The call and code of Christian conduct

To be a Christian means to be a follower of, a believer in, and a disciple of Jesus Christ. It means He is your Lord and Savior. He is your God and there are no others before, beside, or after Him. He is the beginning and the end. We do not necessarily know what all of that means when we come to Him. When we come to Jesus, nothing changes in us physically, mentally, or emotionally. The change is spiritual. (Stay with me here). When we pray a genuine prayer of repentance, understanding we are separated from God forever because of our sin unless we, through Jesus, are reconciled to God, and ask Jesus to forgive us, save us, and be our Lord, we are given the promise of the Holy Spirit - the third person of the trinity. That experience can be very emotional. Those emotions can linger for a day, a week, or longer. However, just like all emotion, it too will subside. When those emotions subside, Satan will try to tell you that you are not saved. Don't' listen to him. It is what we do after that decision and prayer that will make the difference in our lives.

My church encourages people to get baptized immediately upon making the commitment to trust Christ as Lord and Savior, but if circumstances do not allow a same day baptism, do it as quickly as possible thereafter. Why? Number 1 it is scriptural. In Mark 16:16 Jesus says : He who believes and is baptized will be saved. Number 2, baptism is an outward expression, public witness, and declaration of an internal belief. Number 3, and of no less importance, Paul reminds us in Romans 6:4 that we were buried with Christ through baptism into death, that just as Christ was raised from the dead by the glory of the Father, even so we also should walk in newness of life. If there is a physical or emotional response, it will not last long. What will last, however is the spiritual reality of the Holy Spirit taking up residency in our hearts. It is the feeding of that new spirit in us that will make all the difference in our new lives ... or not! When you submit to that new spirit inside your heart, a transformation begins to take place. Feeding the

Holy Spirit living in us, is on us! Walking in that newness of life means taking on new actions. Actions like spending time alone with our Lord and Savior in prayer and study of His word. Actions like spending time with other believers in prayer, service, and fellowship as part of a local church. Actions that cause us to be transformed by the renewing of our minds with the things and knowledge of God and not conforming to the this world any longer. Learning to live according to His Word and not the world. It takes zero effort to live according to the worlds ways. It takes effort to walk with Christ. That is the commitment we make to Him when we ask Him to be our Lord and Savior. We cannot know Him as Savior without submitting to Him as Lord.

1)   Read 2nd Corinthians 5:17 - fill in the blanks.

Therefore if any man be in _____, he is a _____ creature; _____ things are passed away; behold _____ things are become _____.

Trusting Christ as Lord and Savior is where we begin the process of becoming a new creation Old things pass away and all things become new. That's not some magical change that just takes place without us knowing it. We become new in Him. He, through His Holy Spirit, teaches us how to live new lives in Him. His spirit in us responds to His words and His will. Knowledge of who He is, abiding in HIS Word is what transforms us. A change will not happen without spending time alone with HIM in His Word, seeking the good part - as Mary, sister of Martha did. We can go to church. We can pray. We can stop behaviors we believe are not exactly Christian. But, unless we are abiding in HIS Word, unless we are transforming our minds with knowledge of Him so He can prove what is that good and perfect will, unless we are seeking that personal relationship with Jesus, the transformation will not take place. Our submission to Him is our new call. Our call is to be conformed in Christ, through Christ, to the likeness of Christ. The Holy Spirit is the teacher, we are the students and if this transformation is going to take place we have to show up for class.

That is how we become new. It cannot be done without the indwelling of His Holy Spirit. That new birth of His spirit in us is what being a born again Christian is. It is a do-over, a second chance, fresh start, a new life. What a gift. What a savior! His Spirit feeds on HIS Word and that's why we have to be in it - DAILY! Knowing Jesus does not just prepare us for death. It does not just keep us from burning in hell for eternity. While that is a great reason for knowing Jesus as Savior, it is much more than that. Knowing Jesus as Lord fits us for life, and an abundant one at that. There are those who live as though we can know Him as Savior but not as Lord. That is extremely dangerous thinking. I believe in order to enjoy Him as Savior we have to know Him as Lord. I prayed for Him to be my savior at age 10. I didn't really know anything about needing a Lord at that age. All I had known all of my young life was that I loved God. I walked away from that experience in my church that night and not one thing in my life changed. At age 16 when I could drive, date, and had discovered the disco joints, church was out of my life. After five years of reckless living, just doing what everybody else was doing, I understood the need for a Savior and a Lord! People ask me if I believe I was saved at age 10. I say "I'm thankful my salvation was not put to the test." I know that I was "saved" from much harm that could have been done to me because of the poor decisions I made from age 16 to 21.

It is easy to be on our "good" behavior at church. It is amazing how different people are away from church. It shouldn't amaze me though because it takes time to be discipled by Christ. The changes that go on inside one's heart takes a while to be manifested in the flesh. When discipling is not being attempted at home, hearts are not being changed. The "old nature" and "things" are not passing away, not to mention the absence of "all things becoming new." After a while, the emotional high that was experienced with salvation (if there was such an emotional experience) subsides and before you know it, being a Christian hasn't made a difference in your life at all. Maybe you start "feeling" like you aren't saved. Maybe you start questioning if you are really a Christian. Then you start questioning God! Is He even real? A "what has He done for me" type of mentality starts to grow. Does that not also parallel a marriage in trouble? The husband and wife are not spending time with one another, the relationship is not being worked on, before you know it, being married isn't making a difference in your life at all. You start questioning your spousal choice. A what does he or she do for me type of mentality starts to grow. After a while you don't "feel" like you love that person anymore. In fact, you question if you ever really loved them. Before you know it you start looking for something else to fill that void.

Friends we must seek to be discipled by Christ. We must develop a personal relationship so we can understand what Jesus meant when He said He came that we might have life and have it more abundantly. The assurance of who we are in HIM, the assurance of our salvation, the joy and contentment we all seek is found in the fellowship with Christ, not a "feeling." The "feelings" are not sustaining. The fellowship with Jesus is where the sustenance happens. That is what submission is all about. When we submit to HIM, we can rest in the knowledge of HIS complete control. Jesus bought us with the price of His life. When we accept that gift, beloved, we become the elect of God. We are His children. He is our Father. He sees us through the righteous blood of HIS Son, our Savior. We die to self and say yes to Jesus as Lord. Having a Lord means submitting to His way, His will, His word. It is a new life. It is a submitted life.

2) Let's look at Colossians 3. Read the entire chapter and answer the following questions:

Paul tells us we were raised with Christ and therefore we need to seek the things which are above, where Christ is sitting at the right hand of God. He tells us to set our minds on things above, not on things on the earth. In verse 5, what are the members (or parts of our earthly conduct) that we need to "put to death?"

_____, _____, _____, _____ _____,

and _____, which is _____.

3) In verses 8 and 9, he tells us to "put off" what behaviors?

_____, _____, _____, _____,

_____ _____ out of our mouth. Do not _____ to one another since you have put off the old man with his deeds, and (vs. 10) have put on the new man who is renewed in knowledge according to the image of Him who created him.

4) Read verses 12 - 13. What behaviors are we to "put on?"

_____ _____, _____, _____, _____,

_____, _____ with one another, and

_____ one another.

5) Does that mean you have to treat your spouse like that too? We automatically treat others with respect, but to bring that kind of conduct home? Is that what we are being told to do? Is that how we submit to one another? Why on earth would we do that? Especially when we might not have that same type of treatment reciprocated? Look at verses 23-25 and complete the following.

And _____ you do, do it _____, as to the _____ and not to men, knowing that from the _____ you will receive the reward of the inheritance; for you serve the _____ Christ. But he who does wrong will be repaid for what he has done, and there is no partiality.

We take on these new behaviors because we serve the Lord Christ. It is from Him that our reward comes, not from the people we are interacting with. Besides, whoever does wrong (that includes you and me if we are the wrongdoers), will be repaid. Our service is to the Lord. Our reward comes from the Lord. Our conduct has to be pleasing to and representative of Him.

Go back to verse 15. It says, and let the peace of God rule in your hearts, to which you were also called in one body; and be thankful. We are called to a particular behavior when we belong to God. We are sons and daughters of the King! Of course our conduct needs to be representative of that. Our spouse's behavior needs to be representative of that too, but we do not have control over that. I can only control what I do. Can you see how this works together for the good of the home, marriage, church, community, country, and world?

6) Read Galatians 5:19-21. Put a check beside the behaviors that are evident of the flesh.

_____ Adultery _____ Fornication _____ Uncleaness _____ Lewdness

_____ Idolatry _____ Sorcery _____ Hatred_____ Contentions

_____Jealousies _____ Dissentions _____ Heresies _____ Envy

_____ Murders _____ Drunkenness _____ Revelries

_____ Outbursts of wrath _____ Selfish ambitions

6) Read Galatians 5:22-23. Put a check beside the "fruits" that are evident of the spirit of Christ which lives in Christians.

_____ Love   _____ Joy   _____ Peace _____ Patience

_____ Kindness _____ Goodness   _____ Faithfulness _____ Gentleness

_____ Self-Control

When we come under God's authority and submit to His will, He requires us to learn and submit to His ways. When we feed the Holy Spirit that lives in us, the fruit of the spirit is manifested in our lives. Scripture (vs. 23) says "against such there is no law." Nothing can come against us when we walk in the spirit. This is the type of behavior we are called to as Christians, inside, and outside of the home! I heard a story one time about a man who said to his friend "I'm getting the impression you might be a Christian." The friend said, "if all you're getting is an impression, I better clean up my act!" The question is do our friends know we are Christians? Is our conduct in church the same as it is at home? Is our conduct with our spouse the same as it is with other people? Is the fruit of God's Holy Spirit manifested in our lives? It can only come from submission to God. He teaches us how to live according to His ways. We have to show up for class! It is the one on one tutoring that makes the difference. Submission is "the call" for the Christian.

Tomorrow we will talk about the "how to" of submission. For the remainder of your time this morning think about what your marriage would be like if you eliminated the behaviors that are applicable to you in Galatians 5: 19-21 and replaced them with the manifestation of the fruits in verses 22-23. Write in your journal how submitting to God might change things in your home.

Day Five – How does one submit?

One of the easiest ways to learn how to do something is to have someone (who knows how to do what you are seeking to do) teach you! A life style of submission should be a no-brainer in our churches. Unfortunately, that is not always the case. That is not the Pastor's fault, by the way! We have to take responsibility for ourselves. If the preacher is preaching and we are sleeping or busy thinking about what we need to get for lunch at the grocery store after church, guess who missed the blessing? As sad as it is to say, I don't think I 'd be too shocked to know the number of people who leave church on Sunday and never crack open their Bible until the following

Sunday. In fact, they might even keep their Bible in the trunk of the car! As previously discussed, if we, as Christians are not reading our Bibles outside of 3 minutes in church on Sundays, how can we expect Christianity to make a difference in our lives? The answer is WE CAN'T!

I had the awesome blessing of being able to see and hear Henry Blackaby, author of Experiencing God, speak at a church in my hometown. He said (and I paraphrase) when we sit down to study the Word of God or when we hear a sermon preached, if we are not taking notes and becoming a student of what God is trying to teach us, we are kidding ourselves! I remember thinking, "take notes?" I sit in Sunday School and hear people admit to not even reading their Bibles, much less take notes on what they are NOT reading! If you know a Christian who is not reading their Bible, you know somebody who's Christianity does not make a difference in their life. Again, most people want the rewards of being saved, but do not wish to have a Lord. We do not like authority unless it is our own!

We live in a world that does not teach us how to live God's way. Our culture influences us to live in direct conflict with God. It is our responsibility as Christians to learn God's ways and to do what we can to influence culture. At the very least, we are to influence our own households. The way we do that has everything to do with submission. We already know, for the sake of this course, the definition we are using for submission is to surrender to the discretion, will, or authority of another person. That person is God. So what are some practical ways to learn the discipline of submission?

- Read your Bible every day. All throughout this course we have talked about having a quiet time discipline. I recommend the morning. Some people use the evening. Whatever works for you, do it! Have a time, in your quiet time, devoted strictly to reading the Bible.

- Prayer time. Have a time, in your quiet time, that you devote to prayer. God communicates to us through His word. We communicate to God through our prayers. It is a two-way relationship. We need to listen to Him and He wants to hear from us.

- Journal. I strongly recommend keeping a journal.

My journals are simple spiral notebooks. There are fancy journals in all the bookstores, but inexpensive notebooks work just fine. It doesn't matter that you are not a "writer." My journals are letters to God and they are for my eyes only. It is incredible to keep a journal and write through a challenge only to go back once the challenge is over, and see what God taught you through it! The journey has been recorded in your journal perhaps without you even realizing it! Powerful stuff!

If you will do these three things, God will teach you anything else you need to know about submission. Another thing I would encourage you to do is to find a mentor (of the same sex of course). Think of someone you know that demonstrates a lifestyle of submission. Go to that individual and ask them to share the elements that make up their spiritual discipline. We can't learn all there is to know about anything overnight. Don't put that pressure on yourself. We can, however, make the decision to begin the journey, incorporate the key elements into our daily routine, and move forward each day. Today's homework is going to be very easy. We are going to practice how to do what was just suggested. For those of you that are already accustomed to having a quiet time, this just gives you an excuse to have another quiet time this morning (I know that won't upset you!). For those who might be doing this for the first time, just go on and surrender your will, discretion, and authority over to these steps and always remember this day as the day you learned how to be submissive! It's a start!

Are you a coffee drinker? Hot tea maybe? I love to pour a cup of hot coffee and make my way to my quiet time "spot." You might want to pour yourself a nice hot cup of drink and find a comfortable place to sit. Have your Bible, pen or pencil, and a notebook with you. I always keep a highlighter nearby to highlight those special verses! Ray likes to sit at his computer in his office and write. Wherever you're comfortable, just sit there and "still" yourself for a moment. Close your eyes and focus on the fact that you are sitting there in God's presence. It is just you and Him, and He is loving it! Start thanking Him for calling you into fellowship with Him. Start thanking Him for creating this day for you to rejoice and be glad in. Thank Him for anything in your life that comes to mind. Spend as much time in prayer and conversation with Him as you feel led to. At the end of that precious and special time, ask Him to prepare your heart, mind, eyes, and ears to hear and see whatever He might have for you in scripture today. Ask Him to interpret the scriptures you will be reading in a way that will be clear for you to understand. Close your prayer time by thanking Him for the privilege of being able to feast on His Word.

Next, read Proverbs 8:17-36. Have your journal ready to write about anything in those verses that really speak to you. That is how God will talk to you! You take as long as you need to read those scriptures. You might read the first sentence and want to write your thoughts down about it. You might read half way through the verses before something really speaks to your heart. Regardless, just take your time and absorb the words of God. He is speaking to you. Those words are life giving to you and me. They are feeding the Holy Spirit inside us. Put yourself into scripture and claim it for your very own. Once you have worked your way through Proverbs 8, and have recorded how you believe those scriptures have spoken to you, you are ready to make more journal entries.

In your journal, record what today's experience has been like for you. I start my journal entries by saying "Good morning God Almighty!" Sometimes I start my entries with "Good morning Holy God, Heavenly Father, Mighty Counselor, Prince of Peace, Lord of Lord, King of Kings!" I want to enter His presence with humility, acknowledging who He is and how thankful and grateful I am to be able to enter into His gates! I want to enter His presence with gladness! I want Him to know how grateful I am that He made a way for me, through His son, my Savior Jesus, to be able to fellowship with Him. I cannot bear the thought of being separated from HIM and I have to praise HIM for making that way for me. After a time of thanksgiving through words on the paper, I might write some more about what I just read and how I feel He was talking to me through scripture about an area of my life. Sometimes I write to Him about what's going on with my marriage (often I write to Him about that!). Sometimes I write about my son and how grateful I am to be his mother. I do not follow any specific routine with regards to my entries, aside from how I start. I just write as my heart leads. You could say "well, I don't really need to write because God knows my heart and thoughts already." You are right, but let me encourage you to do it anyway because something very powerful happens when you journal your heart to God. I can't explain it and certainly do not understand it. I just know what it has done for me for all of these years. What a blessing to be able to go back and look at my journals and see from whence I've come!

Maybe this exercise today was a defining moment in your life, maybe it wasn't. The important part to realize is you made a step in submission today. You submitted your time to doing this when you could have been doing something else. You submitted to following these directions. Most importantly, your actions showed your submission to God - His Authority, Discretion, and Will. By you having this quiet time this morning, you were saying "I come to you God. I submit myself and my time to you. I understand you are God and I am not. I have heard you through your Word this morning. I have written down, to the best of my understanding, what you are saying to me. I will try to live accordingly." That is how simple submission is. In week eight we talked about surrender, trust, obedience, and accepting Gods vision for life as our vision for our lives. This is how you put it together. You spend time in His word just like you have this morning. You spend time sharing your heart with Him in prayer, just like you have this morning.

You spend time taking notes and making journal entries, just like you have this morning. You will not forget what happened to you today. You will likely ponder your quiet time experience all day long, and then some. When you consistently put together days like today, submission becomes a lifestyle.

As God shapes our heart, mind, spirit, and emotions with His way and will, submission to Him, for His purpose, becomes our desire. The rewards are immeasurable, the benefits immense. Friends, submission is so much more than something a wife does with her husband. Submission is the key that unlocks the door to the abundant life Jesus promises. I pray you have seen submission in a different light. I pray what you have studied this week will encourage you to start developing a lifestyle of submission. Without it, you will miss the rewards God so desperately wants to bless you and your family with. A decision against this lifestyle does not just affect you. It affects your family. It affects the Christian community and it affects the world. When the world does not see any benefit in being a Christian because Christians live life the same way everyone else does, a decision against a submissive lifestyle affects the world. I don't know about you, but I do not want that on my shoulders. I will close this morning with scripture to encourage and remind us all that we must strive to live lives that are worthy of our calling and mindful of the price that was paid for them.

> Ephesians 4:1-5   I, therefore, the prisoner of the Lord, beseech you to walk worthy of the calling with which you were called, with all lowliness and gentleness, with longsuffering, bearing with one another in love, endeavoring to keep the unity of the Spirit in the bond of peace. There is one body and one Spirit, just as you were called in one hope of your calling; one Lord, one faith, one baptism; one God and Father of all, who is above all, and through all, and in you all.

AMEN! Next week, as we end up this study, we are going to visit the rewards of living lives that are worthy of our calling and being ever mindful of the price that was paid for them. When Paul exhorts us in these scriptures to walk with lowliness, gentleness, longsuffering, bearing with one another in love, and endeavoring to keep the unity of the Spirit in the bond of peace, he is not just talking about doing that with people at church. He is talking about that kind of conduct with everybody. Friend, you practice that conduct as a lifestyle at home with your spouse and your children, the rest, as I like to say, "is a piece of cake!" Can you just imagine what this world would be like if Christians loved and lived like this? Guess who it starts with? I look forward to exploring the rewards of this type of life with you as we conclude our study together next week.

WEEK
Eleven
The Reward

Well, we have come to the end of our journey. It is not the end of our journey with Christ, just the end of the class. It is a class that Ray and I have taken over and over. You might want to consider doing the same simply because something new can be learned each time you take it. We have come a long way. In just ten short weeks we have taken a look at where we have come from and the influences that helped shape who we have become. We have looked at just some of God's truths and realized how many false images have been in our past. We have studied God's truths and been challenged to live accordingly. We have looked at our schedules and priorities and prayed for God to purge us of all that would stand in our way or keep us from living for Him. We have even explored the wonders of submission.

This week we are going to look at some of the magnificent rewards that come from living life in fellowship with God. As you continue on your journey, you will discover rewards that will be specific to you and your family. Your life will testify to God's glory and goodness. As your life takes on that new look, your family will be a witness to others. As our lives exalt Christ, He will draw people to Him. Everybody wants what they perceive to be a "good thing." There is absolutely nothing that can compare, in my opinion, to the marital relationship ordained by God. Second to that is the Christian home, as it is ordained by God. I do not claim to have it all conquered. I also admit to being vulnerable, at any given moment, to the wiles of the adversary who seeks to destroy. Therefore, I purpose in my heart daily to stay on the right path through all of the ways I have tried to communicate in this study. You see, as much as I believe what I have told you, and as much as I have attempted to live the truths I have learned and shared, I know I could get off the right path at the very next curve, and there will surely be a next curve. As of this writing, I am 62 years old. Ray and I are approaching our 35th anniversary. I hope we are only half way through. We hope the rewards we are about to share with you, are only half of the ones we will know by the time our life on this earth is over. If, however, I should be called home today, I can honestly tell you, I have no regrets. That, my sweet friends, is a wonderful reward in and of itself.

Much of what you will read this week will be our story. It may hold no appeal to you at all. It is the life we live. It is the life of ordinary people who try to live in fellowship with HIM, learning and living His truths, as best as we can understand them. There are those, no doubt, that are much more spiritual, have much more education, more money, more material possessions, and may very well look at our lives and think we are lacking something. If there is a way of life that is better than the one we live, I trust God will lead us to it. Unless or until then, I no longer ask "is this all there is?" I love my husband. I love our son. I love our family. We invite you into our home and marriage this week. If you are drawn to any of these rewards, know that it is Christ we are lifting up. As He draws us all closer to Him, may we all praise His Greatness.

Day One – Freedom to be who, what, where, and when God calls you to be

Can you imagine waking up tomorrow morning, when your body is rested, with no place in particular to be, no deadlines to meet, no schedules choking you? The most pressing thing on your mind is that you need to get to your quiet time spot. In your quiet time, you are able to stay with God until He "releases" you from your time together. After that, you shower, dress, have breakfast, and go about your day. In the evening, the family enjoys a nice meal, and everything is in peaceful order. As the night-time routine progresses, the family is in harmony. Instead of everyone going to their own rooms and doing their own thing, the family plays a board game, has Bible study, or maybe just sits around and talks. Whatever, there is healthy communication and laughter going on. As time for bed rolls around, the family prays together and shares their heartfelt concerns with each other. They pray for each other and for the family as a unit.

1) Can you imagine that type of lifestyle? Explain your answer.

Since completing the first edition of this book in 2004, I have revised it many times. Our lives have changed drastically since the first writing. In 2004, our son Mark was 16, a sophomore in high school, Ray was in business for himself as a mortgage broker, I worked for him, our poodle

Buffy was 12 and spent most of his days on his pillow under my desk as I worked and wrote. Life was good. Finances were in order and we thought we were right on schedule for retirement. Mark would be going off to college in a couple of years. Ray and I were looking forward to being able to travel as time and opportunity allowed. I was so blessed to be able to work from home and be home for Mark from the time he was 5 years old. I purposefully stopped what I was doing every day (with very few exceptions) before he got home from school and made sure he had the warm chocolate chip cookies and glass of milk waiting for him. We would spend time talking about his day and then he would get on with his homework as I would get back to my work. At 5:00 or thereabouts I'd stop work and start dinner. We always had dinner together. All was well inside our home and I was extremely content with much peace and joy in my heart. Things change! Our world was somewhat shattered in 2008. If you remember, there was a mortgage crisis in America. We had a mortgage company. When the lending dried up, so did our business. Retirement plans were tossed to the wind and it's taken quite a while to recover financially. From then until now we've experienced many ups and downs. Life goes on. Mark is now grown and married to our beautiful daughter-in-love. The point is, all of us experience change. The only thing that doesn't change is God. Through all of life's changes, He continues to be my source of contentment, peace, and joy. That, my friend, is a reward.

God is all about freedom. I have truly learned I am free to be who God calls me to be in Him. I do not have to conform to an image the world has for me. My circumstances do not have to dictate how I live. God paints the vision of the world He intends us to live in through His word. I am free to be what God has called me to. I am not only talking about being saved and receiving the inheritance of an everlasting life in the presence of God. I am talking about the privilege of having been created a woman. I am talking about the blessing of being a wife, and the reward of being a mother. Whether He called me or allowed me to be a wife and mother makes no difference. I am both. As I search scripture, I find meaning, purpose, privilege, position, and reward in those things. As a result of that knowledge, I was able to turn my focus away from what I thought I could do better than my husband. I started to focus on how to do well in, and according to, the image God had for a wife. The instruction that Paul and Peter gave in their epistles to the churches still serve well in the church of God today because it is instruction from God. I know tragedy could strike and our happy little world could be disrupted tomorrow, in fact, tragedy did strike. But that doesn't change who or what God has called us to. We are very happy and very free to live in His calling.

When you have enjoyed the freedom of being who and what God calls you to be, the natural progression is the freedom to be where He calls you, when He calls you. I often tell people, God doesn't do all of this just to bless you and let you live a life unto yourself. No, His commission is for us to GO where He leads, when He wants. This type of life is just the beginning. It is just to get us to the point we can go out as a family and minister to other families. This life is not the end-all. It is the beginning-of-all. We are free to live at peace with one another. We are free to live in harmony in the family order and role assignments ordained by God, and it doesn't matter what people, inside or outside of the church think about it.

We have experienced the reward of living inside the family we believe God has ordained. Ray and I, even with all of our many imperfections, have experienced, and continue to experience, the rewards of living inside the marriage we believe God has ordained. Men, you need to understand what I am about to share (especially in the light of 1st Peter 3: 7-8) It is a huge priority for most women to seek security, wanting to make sure everyone and everything is taken care of. She doesn't do that to put you down. She does it because a woman has to be "safe" and "secure." In fact, most of the women I know will do most anything to insure her and her children are safe and secure in life, even if it means overstepping her husband. Now, she would much rather find that safety and security in knowing that she can trust you to love her and take care of her and the children. But, if she cannot trust you for that, and if she has not been able to turn that insecurity over to God, she will do whatever she has to, to survive in what she perceives is safe and secure. A reward for the life this study has attempted to lead us to will produce a wife who is secure (and at total peace) with the husband being the head of the household. Believe it or not, she really does not want the headship position, and she wasn't engineered for it. The position is yours. You were engineered for it. If you don't accept your responsibilities, she will. That cheats the family and is outside of God's perfect will. It is very liberating for both husband and wife, when she realizes she doesn't have to be in control because he accepts his responsibilities for and to his family, and is accountable to God for them. The truth is, we are accountable to God for what He calls us to do, whether we obey HIM or not. Obedience brings the reward, disobedience brings about the consequence.

I shared with you in an earlier lesson that God taught me I needed to love Ray and depend on God, not depend on Ray and only love God. Learning to trust God has taught me to depend on Him. The same thing applies to both husband and wife. Both need to depend on God, and love their spouse. Meeting the Master every morning sitting or bowing at HIS feet, and developing that relationship with Him has made all the difference in our lives. Our path has not always been easy. We are not in an easy season right now. But we are confidently in HIS care and that makes all the difference. When God took me from working outside the home, (which for me equated to being submissive to a boss, slave to a paycheck, and neglectful of my family), we had no idea what the plan was or how we were going to live. As a result of being obedient to God's call for me to be home, we initially suffered a financial setback. As a result of the setback, Ray changed jobs. God took him to a totally new area of work. He was securely employed in a job that he didn't like, but it had benefits and a paycheck attached to it. Even though we were not able to make ends meet, we still felt secure. That security was a false sense of security because it was based on a paycheck, not the real Provider of life.

Falling further and further behind we really didn't know what we were going to do. God put an opportunity in front of Ray to go into the mortgage business. Even though he had a finance background, he really had very little knowledge of the mortgage industry. To make matters even more scary, it was a straight 100% commissioned sales job. After he had been on the job for some time, I learned he was so nervous he actually got sick in the restroom on his first day. Praise God, Ray persevered. Eventually, God led us to work together in our own business. We were blessed with much freedom to be home while we were raising our son. The blessing of not having to get up every morning and make a mad dash out the door to a place we didn't want to be, with people we didn't want to be with, for a salary we couldn't make ends meet with, was something we will always be grateful for. One of my greatest and fondest blessings from that season of life, was not having to call a boss to say I couldn't come into work if Mark was sick and couldn't go to school. Or if it was a snow day and schools were closed, I loved being able to stay at home with him, having the freedom to be "mom" without having to ask anyone's permission! As a special treat, he and I would have snow day dates! Every time it snowed and there was no school, we would go to Cracker Barrel on a lunch date! We were free to be who, what, where, and when God called us!

That was the framework God established for us during that season of our lives. We are in a different season now. When we took Mark to college (Liberty University in Lynchburg Virginia) on August 14, 2007, and got in the car to come back home, without him, it was precisely at that moment we could sense the winds of change. We cried for months. We were not sad because we had built our whole lives around our son. We were not sad because we had forgotten about our relationship while we were raising our son. We were sad because we loved "the three of us" and the reality is, the three of us as we knew and loved it, was over. As happy as we were for Mark, and as normal as it is for children to grow up and leave the nest, it still hurts. It marks the end of a way of life. Shortly after that, the mortgage business took a nose dive. I can remember waking up one morning thinking "one month our son is gone, the next month our business is gone! What are we going to do now?" It literally happened that fast. That was the beginning of a valley journey. Whether it is a mountain top or valley, we've learned the life we live is a gift God has given to us and we continue to seek who, what, when, and where HE calls us to be.

1) Based on what you have read today, what do you think it means to be free to be who, what, when, and where God calls you to be.

2) Who, in your opinion, has God called you to be?

3) What, in your opinion, has God called you to?

4) When, in your opinion, has God called you to a specific thing and what was it?

5) Were you able to do that thing He had called you to, when He called you? Explain your answer.

6) Are you, in your opinion, where God wants you to be right now? Explain your answer.

7) Read Jeremiah 29:11-14. Personalize that scripture. What do you think about the fact that God has thoughts/plans for you? What do you think God sees as a future and a hope for you? What "captivity" do you think He might have to bring you back from? What does it mean to seek and search for God with all your heart?

The God we serve, the one and only true living God, is all about life giving freedom! Spend the remainder of your time today pondering the freedoms you might come to know if God had His way with you.

Day Two – Freedom to enjoy who, what, when, and where God calls your spouse

Perhaps you are already noticing changes in your spouse. If you will recall there has been nothing in this study that has required you to ask your spouse to change. Hopefully, you have been so focused on your own sweet walk with Jesus that you've not had time to think about what your spouse is or is not doing. There is TREMENDOUS freedom that comes when we understand we are not responsible for our spouses, we are responsible to them!

I can distinctly remember a conversation Ray and I were having years ago right smack dab in the middle of a marital crisis. I am not sure when we learn our spouses are not perfect, but I am sure we all learn that. We were going through a painful challenge in our marriage. As I prayed through that situation, God taught me the most important thing I have learned about my husband. He taught me that Ray, just like me, had to have the freedom to make his own mistakes. In that lesson, God stressed that when one spouse sins against the other, both are faced with a challenge. The one who sinned has to seek forgiveness to be free from the bondage of the sin, and the one sinned against has to forgive if they want to continue being rightly related to God (Matthew 6:15). If either person decides not to seek or give forgiveness, new problems surface. Forgiveness is something we can all seek and give. Redemption is not. It is only the blood of Christ that can redeem us. It was that situation that taught me Ray was accountable to God for Ray, and I was accountable to God for me. That was the night Ray was totally released by me to God. He was free to grow sin lose or win. Instead of me fussing at him any longer, I saw him just like I saw me - a sinner saved by grace! I began praying for him more and yelling at him less. God did not appoint us to be each other's conscience. The Holy Spirit is more than capable of getting a message across and He doesn't need my help! Ray became free to be who God called him to be.

I have watched him become a new man. His freedom has not only benefited him, it has blessed me as a wife and us as a family. When I got out of God's way, and concentrated on becoming who and what God was calling me to, God had complete access to Ray, and Ray had total freedom to become what God created him to become. Guys, please seek God in the things He calls you to and holds you responsible for. Please do not be deceived by thinking your reward or consequence is solely to be found in your wife. Your reward, just like hers, is to be found in Christ. Remember the scripture? Colossians 3:24? There is a much higher level of accountability we all face. It is important for all of us to realize that. It is also vital for us to realize our spouse is not more accountable to us than they are to God. While husbands and wives should be and need to be accountable to one another, each of us has the primary responsibility of answering to God, even if the other one does not like that. We all have to be free to be who God calls us to be. When we try to control each other, we are continually in God's way. Then we have the nerve to cry out to God because our spouse won't be what they are supposed to be! Of course they won't be! We've been trained to try and please, (or silence!) our spouse. Our eyes and hearts aren't where they're supposed to be.

I had to ask myself "Robin, if you really believe God's perfect plan for the family to function in its fullest blessing is when you are in obedience to the order of God, Man, Wife, and Children, are you willing to answer for your disobedience in not living that order?" My answer was no. I did not want to be responsible for what my family did not become because of my disobedience to what I knew God had ordained. I don't think anyone wants to be responsible for what their family does not become. I took what I knew and started living it. I got out of God's way. I have tried, and continue to try, to spend so much time learning what God wants to teach me, that I do not have time to focus on what I think Ray needs to do. I have totally relinquished my husband to God. Truly old things have passed away and behold, all things have become new. They have become new, not perfect. We still have our challenges, but they are new challenges. God has established our marriage and our home. Both of us are at peace with how we interpret the male and female role assignments in scripture and we try to live accordingly. That has put order and respect in our marriage and home. Ray is totally free to be who, what, when, and where God calls him to be. My son and I respect him as the leader of our family. Best of all he has developed a beautiful and very personal relationship with Jesus Christ. Nothing soothes my soul more than to see him reading his Bible, having his quiet time, and see him on his knees in prayer. When I know his authority and strength is found in Christ and Christ alone, I am at peace. Ray's obedience gives me peace.

God has so marvelously taught me that the security I seek can only be found when my husband and I are obediently fulfilling His call for our marriage. Nothing can compare to the security and peace I know in my heart when I see Ray on his knees before our Lord. Nothing warms my heart more than to stand face to face with my husband, holding hands, praying together for each other and our family. There is something powerful about facing him, holding his hands, bowing our heads, and hearing him pray his heart language to God. At that moment, he is humble and he is leader. That is security. God blesses our family through him. That could have only happened as a result of God's Holy Spirit working in both of us, teaching us who we are in Him.

We've not met a married couple that has not experienced some degree of shared selfish destruction. I don't know how long it takes to build the trust that says "you can relax, I have no intentions of hurting you any longer." I just know what it takes to build that trust and, at times, we both fail miserably. Fortunately, as we talk about our lives, and pray through our struggles, we share the perfect bond of love through Christ and that cements our hope in each other. I have so enjoyed watching Ray being transformed into the man he has become. I no longer struggle with many of the things I used to. I am so thankful Ray opens himself up to God. He has taught me how to love. He has taught me how to listen. He has been such a wonderful father to our son and what a pleasure it has been to witness that relationship. He had no role model. He has had to fight all of his life for a better way. His fight ended when He met our Lord. Mark and I are so blessed he finds his delight in Christ. He loves us and it shows in all that he does. All of this has come about because he is free to be who, what, when, and where God has called him to be.

1) Think of your own situation. Would you say you and your spouse are experiencing the freedom of becoming who, what, when and where God has called you? Explain.

2) What do you envision God wants for you and your spouse?

3) What do you think has to happen for that vision to become a reality?

4) What would be the ideal in your heart for your family?

Instead of me giving you scripture today, I want you to search the Bible and try to align the answers you have just given to these three questions with scripture. If you can find scripture to confirm your answers, you can rest in knowing you are in God's will. Fix God's Word in your heart and mind and watch your lives become a testimony to it! How can I back that statement up with scripture? Psalm 37:4

Day Three – Freedom to be "One" with your spouse in God

1) And the two shall become one ... Matthew 19:5. What does that mean? Look up Genesis 2:22-25. I know we looked at these verses earlier in the course. Now that we have gotten to the end, what do these verses say to you?

2) Read Matthew 19:3-6. What do you think Jesus means when He says "therefore what God has joined together, let not man separate?"

3) Who and what can separate a man and his wife? (This is not a trick question, there are many who's and what's - how many can you list?)

I believe one of the main reasons we have so many divorces is because when a couple gets married, they have no idea what becoming "one" means. Becoming one goes way beyond making love with your spouse. It encompasses a oneness in mind, spirit, heart, emotion, and body. There are many things that can separate couples mentally, spiritually, emotionally, and physically. I would encourage you to seriously pray over the who's and what's that are specific to your marriage. If you can eliminate the influence that those things and people have on your relationship, you will find that being "one" has many freedoms to enjoy.

One of the most serious influences that can come between a man and woman is if one or the other (or heaven forbid, both!), never fully leaves home! What do I mean by that? Jesus said "for this reason ..." in Matthew 19:5. What reason was He talking about? Go back to Genesis 2:23-24. In verse 23 Adam said: "this is now bone of my bone, and flesh of my flesh; she shall be called Woman because she was taken out of Man" (vs. 24) therefore (for this reason) a man shall leave his father and mother and they shall become one flesh. Could the "reason" be that she is his completer? Doesn't it make sense that together, through God, we are everything we are supposed to be? We spend untold energy beating each other up over our differences, when we should be thankful we are engineered to cover all the bases!

God has given us the freedom to be one with each other. A lot of people don't understand that, especially some parents. Parents need to understand God's plan themselves, for themselves. Then they need to let their children go. As well intentioned as they might be, parents can be one of the who's that separate a man and wife. How? By not respecting that the couple is now a family in its own right, so they meddle, for lack of a kinder word. We, as parents, spend 18 years (maybe longer) training our children to come to us with any and everything. It is very difficult to stop that as they get older and when they get married. (I am about to find out how well I take my own advice as my son is soon to be married!) Of course we want them to always come to us for whatever type of help they might need and we might be able to offer. However, there is a difference in enabling a negative situation, and helping our child and their mate seek a resolve with a challenge. For example, your child comes to you and says "you wouldn't believe what she did this time!" A healthy way to handle that is to tell your son you would be happy to talk with both of them about it. The unhealthy way to handle that is to feed the negative and tell him what you would do to straighten her out!

We can be our own "who" that separates ourselves. Husbands and wives separate themselves all the time. The pastor that meant so much to Ray and I preached a sermon one time on promotions in life. He talked about how we are promoted from one stage of life into the next, all the time. For instance, we are promoted from pre-school to kindergarten, elementary school to middle school, middle school to high school, high school to college, college to career, being single to being married, being married without children to being married with children, etc. etc. Each step of the way can be a problem if we do not grow with the promotion. Your behavior should change as each promotion brings on new responsibilities. Obviously you do not act the same way in high school that you acted in pre-school. When you get married you do not act (or should not act) the same way you did when you were single. With each new promotion there comes new expectations and responsibilities. When we do not grow with each position, we are not giving that stage of life the priority we should. When husbands and wives do not make those positions priority, separations occur. I am not working on being one with my spouse if I am more concerned about things and relationships outside of my home, than I am with the relationships inside my home. Those things and relationships could be anything from work, to church, to other people, to social concerns. You might be thinking I am over the edge on this. I might be. I just know the damage that is done to a marriage when the marital relationship is not given the priority it needs and God's word demands.

There are two things that could change every marriage for the better, instantaneously. One is sweet, encouraging, and pleasant words. The other is praying together. I am shocked at the number of Christian couples that do not pray together. Praying together is fundamental to our faith. Let me tell you what we miss. Spiritually we miss out on the closeness that comes from praying together. When you pray with your spouse, you get to hear their heart. I have already shared with you the security and peace that comes over me when I stand facing my husband, holding his hands as we pray together. When you pray with your spouse, you know they care, you can detect compassion, and it keeps the lines of communication open. When husbands and wives do not pray together, it is very easy for there to be a breakdown in communication.

Mentally, we miss out on being "one" in mind. We do not think the same on many things. That is not always bad, but no communication and sharing of those differences can cause us to take different paths. Before long, we realize we have nothing in common. When we communicate with one another, even if we do not agree, we can at least understand and respect where the other opinion is coming from. Being on the same page mentally allows for a type of oneness that can only be known between a husband and wife. It is an intimate oneness that allows you to know what the other is thinking. It is a silent type of communication that makes you the most precious person in each other's life. There is not another relationship between two people like it.

Emotionally we miss out on the support we need, maybe just to make it through the day. When we are in tune with one another's emotions, we can use our emotions to build the relationship and bring honor to God. So often we accuse the other of "making me feel like........" and you can fill in the blank. You read in the first lesson that I fell in love with Ray because of the things he did and the way he made me feel. I also wrote that I fell out of love with Ray because of the things he did and the way he made me feel. Being one with your spouse means you learn those emotions and use them to build the relationship, not destroy it. If I do something that upsets Ray, he needs to tell me about it and I need to stop it. I will share that while it works both ways, I have no control over what he does to make me feel a certain way, but I do have control over how I react. It is so important to learn how to manage those emotions. When you do, you enjoy a oneness that makes you feel emotionally safe and secure with one another, not torn up and ripped apart.

When you are spiritually, mentally, and emotionally "one" with each other, all of the ingredients are right and perfect for a physical oneness. Physical intimacy becomes a bond that says you are not only one with each other, you are each other. It takes us back to Adams proclamation that says "you are now bone of my bone and flesh of my flesh." All of what I have described in the last couple of paragraphs is the type of oneness I believe God intends for husbands and wives to enjoy. It is the type of oneness that produces healthy families. It is the type of oneness that produces Godly offspring - which is why God says we are to be one anyway.

4) Read Malachi 2:14-15. We looked at these scriptures in another lesson. In the context of "oneness" what is your interpretation of this message?

Can you see how it all works together? Can you see that God wants us as one for our own benefit and that of the next generation? I look at the world (even inside the church) and see deterioration. I look at the world, and at couples inside the church and see husbands and wives dealing treacherously with one another. Something is terribly wrong with that. How are we going to win the world for Christ when we can't even "live" Christ in our homes and marriages? God sends His message through the prophet Malachi as a warning to protect the sacredness of the vow. It is our promise to God. It is our commitment to God. In verse 14 he talks about the wife as companion and by covenant. That says to me two commitments are made when getting married. One commitment is to the person, the other is to the marriage. We owe it to God by commitment, our spouse by covenant, and our children by complying to Gods Word to become "one" with each other. The rewards are tremendous. The consequences are devastating.

5) Read Malachi 2:16. What does God say about divorce?

6) Why does He hate it?

7) What is His remedy for avoiding it?

If we are to take heed to our spirits and that is to keep us from dealing treacherously with our spouses, it makes sense to me that our focus needs to be at home. You cannot have oneness in your marriage if it is not an intentional focus. Being one does not mean you are in total harmony 100% of the time. It means you are in harmony most of the time and when you are not, you are in total respect of one another. It also means you are very secure in the relationship. Ray and I are in total agreement that God's order for the family is God first, then man, woman, children. We believe we have total equality in creation, grace, salvation, and inheritance. We have been given specific role assignments to help us relate to each other the way it works best in our home environment. With both of us in total agreement, it has provided an extremely safe and secure environment for our son to grow up in. While our son is not perfect, he has shown signs through the years of being "godly offspring." We believe that is a testimony to the word of God.

Finally, while Ray and I are still growing in this area of becoming one, we believe it has been worth every struggle we have endured because of the baggage we know our lifestyle has eliminated for our son to have to carry with him into adulthood. Does that mean he will not have problems? Absolutely not! Does that mean he will always follow the straight and narrow path of life? Not necessarily. That is his decision. We just know that we have tried to intentionally provide what we believe is the biblical mandate for the best environment for him to grow in. We might not know this side of glory if that proves true. Our desire continues to be that we will live all the days fashioned for us by God, enjoying the "oneness" He calls us to. Spend the remainder of your time this morning writing in your journal about aspects of your marriage you would consider to be evidence of growing in oneness.

Day Four – Freedom to live life God's way

We live in a world of diversity. It is a great time to be alive. We live in a country full of freedom to become and do whatever we want. I believe it is the best country in the world! I am so thankful to our countless men and women of the military who paid the ultimate sacrifice so I can live in this freedom. Greater than that freedom, however, is the freedom that I know as a born again, saved by the blood of Jesus Christ, sanctified and set apart child of God! No matter what is going on in my life or in this world, I will always belong to and be free in Him! That is a reward. As free as I am to live life God's way, He will not attack me with the knowledge it takes to live that way.

1) Read Matthew 7:7-8. What are the three instructions and what are the three promises from Jesus?

We can't live it if we are not learning it. We can't learn it if we are not reading it. We won't experience it if we are not experiencing, building, or developing that relationship with Jesus. I hear people talk a lot about having "devotions." I make no judgment on that and highly encourage it. I will go out on a limb here and say a devotion might be good but a relationship is better. What is the difference? One is the way you spend your time, two is the result.

I used to have a devotion that went something like this. I would read out of a devotional book. There was usually a scripture and a little commentary that went along with it. It might take me all five minutes to read. I would say a little prayer and that was my devotion. When I was introduced to the idea of a quiet time, it went something like this. I had to pray before I started reading from the Bible that the Holy Spirit would open my eyes, ears, heart, and mind to whatever He wanted me to learn that day from God's Word. I was also to pray that God, through His Holy Spirit, would allow me to understand what I was reading. Then I had to read scripture until something really impressed me. Then I had to write about what I read and how I believed it was to be interpreted. You see, I can have a devotion and not even talk to God, much less listen for Him to talk to me. But when I have a quiet time, I am actively asking, seeking, and knocking with an expectation of hearing from God. That is an intentional relationship!

As I have learned through the years to sit at the feet of Jesus and be taught by Him - the Word in the flesh- He has become life itself for me. He is the reason my marriage is what it is. He is the reason our home life is what it is. The greatest fear I know is the fear of what life would be without Him. I am eternally relational with Him and eternally grateful to Him for calling me into fellowship with Him. I am free to live God's way. If you read further in Matthew 7:13-27 you will learn that the way to life is narrow and difficult and few find it; you will learn that you will know people by their fruits; you will learn that not everyone who says Lord, Lord will enter the Kingdom of Heaven, just those that do the will of the heavenly Father; and finally you will learn that it is wise to build your house on the Rock - Jesus.

2)   Read Matthew 7:24-27.

     What does Jesus say about the person who hears His sayings AND DOES THEM?

3) Why does He liken them to a wise man who built his house on the rock? (a strong foundation, the foundation of Jesus as the Rock?)

4) What does Jesus say about the person who hears His sayings and DOES NOT DO THEM?

5) Why does He liken them to a foolish man who built his house on the sand?

Friends, the rains, floods, and winds are the same for all of us! Destructive things, temptations, selfish desires, bad attitudes, distractions, tragedies, hardships, periods of discouragement, difficult people, responsibilities of life, etc., etc., are those rains, floods, and winds. It is called life! The wise ones will hear His sayings and do them, and when those things come, the house will not fall because it has been built on the rock. The same is not true for the one who hears His sayings and does not do them. Those things will come, the house will fall, and great will be that fall. Take the time right now to think about a family you know personally that has suffered the tragedy of divorce. If my guess is right, it didn't take you long to think of some one. Perhaps it was even you. We are all free to live God's way, but very few will choose it.

We have friends and are familiar with people that have suffered from not building their homes on the foundation of Christ. As life has progressed, we have seen some of them divorce and those that have not, we have seen destructive things continue to tear at their home and relationships. Every time we witnessed this as we were raising our son, we used it as a time of learning and a time of teaching him how those situations bear testimony to the word of God. It is as important to see how scripture is fulfilled when we do not obey it, as it is to show how it is fulfilled when we do obey it. Often we say "but for the grace of God, there we go!" And just because we are enjoying the blessings today, doesn't mean we have a free pass for tomorrow. We stand a better chance of getting those blessings when we show up for the relationship. And let me just add, that as I have talked about enjoying the blessings throughout this entire study, the blessings are not the main concern. The honor and glory that is brought to God by living life in obedience to Him is the main concern. I say that because blessings might not always look like what we think they should. Blessings can be disguised and that is just one more reason we need to thank **HIM** for everything, even when it doesn't make sense. Job's life proves that and God is no respecter of persons.

We have the freedom to live life God's way and there is no better way to live it. It has to be intentional though. We do not live it just because we have prayed the sinner's prayer. We do not live it because we took a walk down a church aisle, became a member, and got baptized. We do not live it because we profess Christianity. We live it because we actively ask for it, seek it, and knock until it is opened to us. A devotion shows we are loyal to an act. A relationship shows we are committed to a person. A good friend of mine who has done this study several times over the past 20 years recently shared that God revealed to her this time that she has been committed to her marriage for as long as she has been married - 54 years. However, she said she realized she had not been surrendered to God's ways in that commitment. She is learning how to surrender to God in her marriage. As we commit to the person of Jesus Christ, as we build that trust relationship, He will most definitely lead us in that surrender.

Spend the remainder of your time this morning writing in your journal about how your relationship with Jesus Christ is affecting your life, or not. Be open to hear whatever He wants to communicate to you about it. Act on His instruction. Resolve to know Him better today. Resolve to learn how to build your house on the Rock.

Day Five – Freedom to hear God say, "Well done my good and faithful servant."

Wow! We have made it to the end. Or should I say the beginning? This is all we have. Depending on how much you have put into this will determine where you will go with it. You can decide it is the end and go back to business as usual, or you can say "I have taken the class now and I am ready to be a Christian husband or a Christian wife and we are committed to allowing God to build our marriage!" This has been my adult Christian life-work. I do not know how this might be elaborated on in years to come. It is my prayer this study has led you to the ONE who makes the difference in your life. I pray that the personal testimony, choices of scriptures, questions/daily exercises, and encouragement to keep a journal has been enough to at least get you moving in the right direction. I greet you on this last day with mixed emotions of joy and happiness! Joy to know we made it to this point, and happiness for what it could mean for you and your family. The best part is yet to come - here on earth and in heaven. We have focused thus far this week on our earthly rewards. Today, we will focus on and close out this course thinking about our eternal reward.

Jesus knew who He was, where He had come from, what His purpose was, and where He was going when He left this earth. Hopefully, we are all learning who we are in Him, what our purpose is, and are totally confidant of where we are going when we leave this earth. It is the Christian belief that when we die and are absent from the body, we are present with the Lord. We go to heaven. We enter into our final rest. Can you just imagine what it would be like to hear God say "well done my good and faithful servant; you were faithful over a few things, I will make you a ruler over many things. Enter into the joy of your Lord!" Of course you will recognize those words as they are taken from the parable of the talents in Matthew 25:21. I do not know if God greets people in heaven like that or not. But at the slight chance He might, I sure want to hear those words. The parable talks of servants taking the talents their Master has given them and turning them into more talents. As the story goes, two servants made great use of what had been given to them and they were rewarded. One servant, however, buried what had been given to him and his master called him a wicked and lazy servant. The master took away what had been given to that servant and gave it to the one who had doubled his talents.

1) Read Matthew 25:29. What does it say about those who have? Who have not?

2) Which one do you want to be?

It is there for the taking! It is up to us. We choose life and blessing or death and cursing.

3) Read Deuteronomy 30:11-20. Paraphrase those verses making them personal to you.

My favorite part of that scripture is found in vs. 19. 'choose life, that both you and your descendants may live, that you may love the Lord your God, that you may obey His voice, and that you may cling to Him for He is your life and the length of your days!' I choose life! He is my life! He is the length of my days! I want to hear His voice, love my God, and cling to Him. I also want a pure heart because Jesus says that the pure in heart will see God!

4) Read Matthew 5:8. What do you think having a pure heart means?

The truth and desire of God is that we choose life and blessing, live in our promised land, practice purity in heart, and get to see God one day. I was created by God, love living in fellowship with HIM, and believe I will spend eternity with HIM. While hearing Him say "well done, my good and faithful servant" would be the icing on the cake, just getting there will be reward enough. Whether I ever actually hear those words or not, it is motivating to me to know I am free to live like I might hear them some day. Let it be said of us that none of how we live is without purpose. I am a servant of God and so are you. He wants us to do well what He calls us to do. He gives us the choice to determine if we will answer that call because He is an all powerful loving and just God who knows that one who serves from the heart makes the best servant. A volunteer turns their call into a labor of love. We show our love for God when we love HIM and keep His commands. I am a wife. I am a mother. I have been called to positions where my influence, good or bad, will affect my descendants. You are a husband and likely a father. What you do, good or bad, in obedience or disobedience to God, will influence generations. The small marks we leave on this earth will affect generations. Who I become affects more than just me. I have a lot more to answer for than just what I didn't learn because of not spending time reading the Bible. The time I spend in God's Word, or the lack thereof, will have a most profound effect on those around me.

We are all free to hear Him say "well done good and faithful servant." He has given us all we need to know what to do and how to do it! What will your decision be? Are you going to take your position as a husband or wife and bring honor to God, or are you going to toss it aside? We can pretend we won't meet Him one day. We can pretend what we are as a wife/ husband is not important and without consequence. We can't pretend the little hearts and minds we influence will not be affected by the way we treat their father or mother. We can pretend our husbands/ wives are the reason we aren't what we could be. We can even pretend they could never be what they should be. The truth is, the truth says different!

Short of spending every minute of every day with you, I couldn't begin to know what you go through daily. God knows what all of our days are like. He fashions everyone we have! He sees us from heaven and considers our works - good or bad.

5)   Read Psalm 33:13-15. How do these verses speak to you?

6) What do you believe God sees when He sees you at work (inside or outside of your home)?

7) What do you believe God sees when He considers your work at church?

8) What do you believe God sees when He considers your work in your relationship with your spouse, children?

9) If God is going to compliment you on being a good and faithful servant, what specifically is He going to compliment you on?

10) What is your promised land and what do you have to obey to reap the promises?

11) Are you willing to do what it takes? _____ yes _____ no _____ not sure

Ray and I enjoyed every minute of being with you. Our prayer is not only that you will find benefit in this for your marriage and family, but that you will be used by God to help others benefit in a stronger marriage and Christian home life. We believe Christians should be the salt of the earth. We believe Christians are the light of the world. We believe we should give light to all who are inside and outside of our homes. Our lights should so shine before men that they will see our good works and glorify our Father in heaven. It is a personal belief that all of that starts inside my home, inside my heart, with my Lord and Savior Jesus Christ. If we get it right at home, we've gotten it right. I have asked you many times throughout this course to spend the remainder of your morning writing about whatever we were talking about for the day. Today I ask you to spend the remainder of your life seeking the One who knows you best and loves you most. "For I know the thoughts I think toward you, thoughts of peace and not evil, to give you a future and a hope. You will seek Me and find Me when you search for Me with all your heart." "Call to Me and I will answer you and show you great and mighty things which you do not know." Jeremiah 29:11-13, 33:3.

WEEK
Twelve
A Time of Sharing

Congratulations! You have now graduated! Well, we may have finished this class, but there are already parts of it I know I need to go back and take over - again, and again, and again. We are never quite where we could be are we? Making progress is rewarding. We know you can look over the last eleven weeks and see areas of change. If you are like us, we know it isn't hard to look over the last eleven weeks and see where more change is needed. In time, with patience and persistence, positive changes happen. Don't give up on yourself. We will make you a promise that we are praying for you. We won't turn down any prayers you want to send our way either! Let's continue to pray for each other.

You may have taken this class on your own. It is designed to take on your own or with a group. If you have taken it on your own, you will still want to answer the questions at the bottom of this page just so you can revisit the things you have learned. If you have taken it with a group, your facilitator may have asked you to be prepared to share some things you have learned at a special time of testimony. Use your time this week to go back through your workbook and record anything in your journal that has been meaningful to you. Come to the last class prepared to share.

There are five questions below. Just like the five day format in previous lessons, spend time answering one question per day.

1. Go back through each lesson. Record anything that you highlighted and write in your journal what you found meaningful about that phrase, thought, or scripture.

2. What is the most important thing you have learned in this class?

3. Has your marriage and your home seen benefits from the things you have learned?

4. Has your quiet time with God improved? Why or why not?

5. Would you recommend this class to other couples? Why or why not?

THE HUSBAND AND WIFE BOOK
Leader/Facilitator Guide

Kudos to you for leading/facilitating a group! This is a guide to help you do that. Of course you can alter/adjust as you see fit based on the dynamics of the group.

Please do not feel like you have to answer all of the questions each week. These are discussion starters. You might even be led to ask other questions based on what was revealed to you during your time in the study for the week. This is a guide. As the weeks progress, you will know your group better than anyone. These questions are designed to help everyone benefit from what God has revealed during the week. There are no right or wrong answers. Decide how long each weekly session will go. Most groups limit the time frame to one and a half or two hours. Suggest to participants to get an inexpensive notebook to aid them on this journey!

WEEK *One*
Introduction

This is a time of introduction ... to each other and to the study. Have everyone introduce themselves and briefly share what they are hoping to get out of this class. Leader/Facilitator, start by introducing yourself and what you hope to get out of the class.

Have everyone read Week One - Introduction. Leader/Facilitator can read out loud and others follow along.

Have everyone read the Table of Contents. Leader/Facilitator can read out loud and others follow along.

Point out that Week Twelve is a time of sharing and testimony. Some groups make this a special time of celebration by sharing a covered dish or pot luck brunch, lunch, or dinner. That might not be possible for your group depending on your meeting venue. What makes this time so special is the sharing that has gone on throughout the previous eleven weeks. You will get to know and learn from each other as you share the things God reveals to you along this journey.

Groups often find it beneficial to agree to the following guidelines:

1. Respect the confidentiality of every member of the group.
2. Unless permission is given to share what someone says, DON'T! Keep it in the group.
3. No husband or wife bashing.
4. Repeat 1, 2, & 3.
5. Pray for each other.
6. Be respectful of each other's time. No one person should dominate the discussions.
7. Commit to doing the work and being at each weekly gathering.
8. If comfortable, share contact information (phone numbers/email addresses) to be used to stay in touch and/or encourage each other through this study.

Close in prayer.

WEEK Two
Am I the only one who feels like this?

Start with prayer.

Each week before discussing the questions, ask participants to review and share one or two highlights that may have spoken to them this week. It could be a phrase, scripture, or something the author shared that they relate to. Ask them to share why it made an impression.

Emphasize this is strictly voluntary. Not everyone will feel comfortable sharing. Once you feel everyone who wants to share has shared, move on to the discussion starters. You don't have to go in order and you don't have to cover all of them. If you are going to cover them all, be mindful of the time you allow for each one.

1) Was there anything in particular that you related to with regards to how much we all experience the same things in our marriages?

2) What are some things we can do to contribute to the "health" of our marriages?

3) Why is it important to be mindful of who you talk to about your marriage?

4) 1st Peter 3:8 tells us to be like-minded (or of one mind), have compassion for each other, to love as brothers (and sisters), to be tender-hearted to each other, and to be courteous to each other. That is oftentimes easier to do with strangers than it is to do inside our own homes with our own family. Why is that and what are some examples of being like-minded, having compassion, loving as brothers, being tender-hearted, and courteous to each other inside our homes - when no one can see us?

5) We talked this week about our manner of speech, who we talk to about our marriages, and who we get advice from. Does God care about any of that? Why or why not?

WEEK Three
In the Beginning ... False Images, Part I

1) What does it mean to be raised under false images vs being raised in the image we are created in?

2) On Day 1 and 2, we looked at what we were like before we got married and answered questions to help us think about why we were like we were. Were you more influenced by the world or by Christ and how did that play out in your dating relationship?

3) Once the dating relationship became a marital relationship, did either of you change and if so what has influenced the changes?

4) Is it important to understand how your spouse was raised? Why?

5) What did you think marriage was going to be like?

WEEK *Four*
When the honeymoon is over ... False Images, Part II

1) What does it mean when someone says "the honeymoon is over?"

2) On Day 1 and 2 we looked at what we are like and why we are like we are now. Does marriage change people? If so, how?

3) If your image of marriage has changed, is it just "your marriage" or is it your image of "marriage in general" that you feel has changed. Explain your answer.

4) The honeymoon is an event - not a lifestyle. Hopefully you have done enough self examination over the last couple of weeks (about yourself and your knowledge of your spouse) to know that "marriage" is not just an extension of "dating" therefore it has to be treated as such. What are some things that are present in a marriage that are NOT present in a dating relationship? Are those "things" irritations or reasons for divorce?

5) We were encouraged on Day 5 to stop focusing on our spouse and spend the rest of this study focusing on our own relationship with God and HIS TRUTHS. Write a promise to yourself that you will pray for your spouse the next time they do something that irritates you instead of getting mad and dwelling on how irritated you are. Write a prayer to God to help you focus on HIM and not the irritation.

WEEK *Five*
What is the truth?

1) Discuss (specifically) how God made man, how he made woman, and what that relationship looked like. Is it still supposed to look that way today? Why or why not?

2) Discuss the fall of man. What happened that made God send Adam and Eve out of the garden of Eden? What part did the serpent play? How do we fall into the same pattern of sin?

3) On Day 2 we looked at our identity as Christians. We were to read Matthew 5, 6, & 7 and see how many of Jesus' sayings we could identify to help us through the storms of life. How many can the group identify?

4) On Days 3 and 4, we looked at our identity as Christian husbands and wives. What spoke to people about their specific identities?

5) Have everyone write in their journals what they think their marriage would look like if they pursued their identities in Christ. How would it effect their home life? The children?

WEEK *Six*
Love, Marriage, Family

1) What is love according to the world? What is love according to God? (1st Corinthians 13:4-8)

2) What is Christ to the church? How does Christ love the church? How does the church love Christ?

3) If the husband is to be to the wife and family what Christ is to the church, and the wife is to be her husband what the church is to Christ, what does that look like inside the marriage and family/home? Really think about this question and have an in-depth discussion about it.

WEEK *Seven*
A Time to Reflect

1) What have you learned about yourself?

2) What have you learned about false images?

3) How does a marriage suffer when God's Truths are not being lived out in the home?

4) Based on what you have learned over the last 7 weeks, would you say you've spent your life living under false images or according to God's truths? Explain your answer.

5) How does a marriage and family benefit by living according to God's Truths?

WEEK *Eight*
Decision Time: Accepting God's Vision for yourself, your marriage, and family

1) How do you surrender yourself or something like a habit, or attitude, or relationship, etc. to God? Ask if anyone would like to briefly testify to something they've successfully surrendered.

2) Discuss trust relationships people have had in their lives - what were the characteristics of that relationship? Discuss untrusting relationships - what made them untrusting?

3) Why is God trustworthy?

4) In Day 3 of Week 8, the author describes obedience in the first paragraph. Read that paragraph out loud. Discuss things that keep people from being obedient. Discuss things that entice people to be obedient.

5) We have no control over other people. How difficult is it to accept your spouse "as is" and focus attention on becoming what God wants you to become?

6) How would you describe your faith and what difference does it make in your life? In your marriage? In your home?

WEEK *Nine*
Priorities

1) One of the biggest challenges couples have to work out is the responsibility of running the household and everything that involves. Quite often that responsibility falls on one person, and that is in addition to also working a full-time job. What are some ways your family shares those responsibilities?

2) On Day Two there is an exercise to help you draw out your week to visualize how you spend your time and what relationship(s) are most important according to the time you devote to it or them. What did your chart reveal to you?

3) Is it important to discern if an activity or area of service or a commitment of time is a prompting of God? Put another way, is it important to determine if the way you are spending your time is something you want to do or something God wants you to do? Explain your answer

4) Have you ever allowed God to take you on a purge? Clear your schedule? Commitments? When your schedule is clear, do you feel a need to fill it up? Discuss your experience in this area.

5) Day Five talks about the connection between priorities and peace. Discuss your interpretation of that as a group. If anyone in the group feels like their lives and homes are at peace most of the time, have them share what their family/relationship priorities are.

WEEK *Ten*
Submission is not a bad word! And it's not just for wives!

1) What is submission? How has it been portrayed in "the world" and in the "Christian world?"

2) Discuss your thoughts on submission, i.e. is it hard to swallow, easy to live, correctly understood?

3) How/why is submission powerful for the Christian?

4) Who does God call us to submit to first? In the family order, what does submission look like? Discuss how difficult (or not) that is to live - and why do you come to that conclusion?

5) Are all Christians called to submission? Explain your answer.

6) On Day 5 the author gives some practical ways to start developing a lifestyle of submission. Discuss the benefits you have seen from implementing these disciplines.

WEEK *Eleven*
The Reward

1) How can one be free to be who and what God calls them to be?

2) How can we help or hinder our spouse from enjoying the freedom to be what God calls them to be?

3) What is "being one" with your spouse? What type of liberty do you need to extend to each other to enjoy all parts of oneness?

4) What does living life God's way look like?

5) If God does say to you "well done my good and faithful servant" what will He be complimenting you on?

WEEK *Twelve*
A Time of Sharing

This is a time to celebrate all that the Lord has revealed, and any progress people feel they have made in their relationship with the Lord and with each other. Some groups plan a potluck or covered dish meal to share. It is meant to be a time of honoring God with stories of things people feel were revealed to them during the previous eleven weeks. To prepare for this celebratory time, everyone should treat week twelve just like they did each week. There are 5 questions for week twelve that will help people reflect on meaningful scriptures, the most important things learned, benefits seen in the marriage and home, and how your quiet time has improved. Encourage those who feel comfortable sharing in front of the group some of the ways they have been affected by this journey.

There is a personal message in the back of the book. Encourage people to reach out to Ray and Robin with any questions or things they would like to share.

PERSONAL MESSAGE

Dear Friends,

Not knowing where you were in your marriage or your heart attitude when you started this journey makes it difficult for us to know where you've ended up. Our prayer is that you have learned some things along the way to make you thirsty enough to keep coming back. It has been our experience this is not a one and done course. Our desire is to see it get into as many hands and hearts as God would see fit.

We are not professional counselors. We are just two people who submitted ourselves and our marriage to God to rebuild what we had torn apart. We have tried to communicate our story and the process He gave us in a way that can help anyone who cares to learn. We will be the first to tell you it is not easy. Being totally honest, a marriage not surrendered to God is even harder.

If you ever want to reach out to us, ask questions, or share your story, we would love to hear from you. We have held these classes in churches where it has been within reasonable travel distance. We have shared testimony in person for classes that have a celebration and time of sharing at the end of the twelve weeks. It is our delight to interact with and hear from people who have testified to God's goodness upon completion of this course. So whether you are doing this on your own, as a wife or as a husband and your spouse is not participating, or whether you are doing this in a small or large group, or even as a church, we would love to participate in some way. Technology makes so much possible these days. If you are interested in an online class, or "zooming" us into your group, let us hear from you. Send an email and let's get the conversation started!

In His love and ours!

Ray and Robin
robin@thehusbandandwifeclass.com

Made in the USA
Middletown, DE
04 September 2020